To Aralyne
With affection
From Tino

American Romanticism and the Marketplace

American Romanticism

AND THE

Marketplace

Michael T. Gilmore

The University of Chicago Press
Chicago and London

Michael T. Gilmore is professor of English at Brandeis University.

The University of Chicago Press, Chicago 60637
The University of Chicago Press, Ltd., London

© 1985 by The University of Chicago
All rights reserved. Published 1985
Printed in the United States of America
94 93 92 91 90 89 88 87 86 85   5 4 3 2 1

Library of Congress Cataloging in Publication Data

Gilmore, Michael T.
    American romanticism and the marketplace.

    Includes index.
    1. American literature—1783–1850—History and
criticism.   2. American literature—19th century—History
and criticism.   3. Romanticism—United States.   I. Title.
PS217.R6G54   1985   810'.9'003   84-23936
ISBN 0-226-29395-5

To Deborah and Emma

Contents

Acknowledgments

I owe many people thanks for having helped me with this book. For the past few years, I have tried out my ideas on students at Brandeis and have benefited from both their agreement and their resistance. Several students in particular spurred me to refine and clarify my thinking: I especially wish to mention Tass Bey, Charles Hatten, Cynthia Jordan, Victoria Minden, Claudine Torchin, and Cindy Weinstein. Various colleagues and friends provided assistance by reading and commenting on sections of the manuscript. I am grateful to Philip Fisher, Winfried Fluck, Eugene Goodheart, Allen Grossman, Leo Marx, Ronald Sanders, Richard Strier, and Brook Thomas for their thoughtful criticism. Michael McKeon and Cecelia Tichi took time from their own projects to give careful readings to troublesome chapters; both made essential suggestions for revision and gave me needed encouragement at a critical time. I am also indebted to Daniel Aaron, Sacvan Bercovitch, Emory Elliott, and Joel Porte, all of whom read the manuscript in its entirety and offered support as well as valuable advice. Two anonymous readers for the University of Chicago Press supplied detailed critiques that included numerous ideas for improvement. Most of all, I would like to thank my wife Deborah Valenze, whose love and understanding sustained me through the writing of this book, even as she completed her own book on English working-class religion. I have dedicated *American Romanticism and the Marketplace* to her and to our daughter Emma, who was considerate enough to be born one day after I returned the revised manuscript to Chicago for copy editing.

Introduction

1832 – 60 econ rev

The American romantic period was the era of the marketplace. Between 1832, when Emerson resigned from the ministry to pursue a career as a literary man, and the publication in 1860 of Hawthorne's fourth and final novel, *The Marble Faun*, an economic revolution transformed the United States into a market society. The revolution began perhaps a decade and a half earlier, and required the Civil War to complete, but it proceeded at its most rapid pace during the very years when the classic works of American literature were produced. Literature itself became an article of commerce at this time, as improvements in manufacture, distribution, and promotion helped to create a national audience for letters. The gentlemanly author who wrote for a like-minded group of equals gave way to the professional who depended for a livelihood on sales of his books to an impersonal public. What I attempt to show in the following pages is that these two developments, the commercialization of society and of culture, profoundly affected the American romantics and had a shaping influence on the themes and form of their art.

Marketplaces, to be sure, have existed since the beginnings of recorded history,[1] and even in the eighteenth century there were few Americans, including those residing on farms, who did not take part in some forms of exchange. But clearly the years from about 1815 to 1860 marked a watershed in the history of the American economy. Before the War of 1812 the marketplace had not penetrated very deeply into the lives of most Americans. The United States was still an overwhelmingly agrarian society with economic activity centered in the home. People commonly worked for themselves as farmers or artisans, producing for use rather than profit. Most depended on their own exertions or on direct reciprocal transactions for necessities like food and clothing. The exchange of goods tended to be local and, in rural areas, often unmediated by money. One farmer might trade a bushel of his wheat for a neighbor's help with his harvesting; another might swap some of his produce for a new pair of boots or the services of a blacksmith. Even when crops made their way to outside markets, they were seldom raised expressly for purposes of exchange. "They were taken from the surplus that was left over after household and community needs had been met."[2] At this early date neither land nor labor was widely regarded as a commodity.

The scale and character of American enterprise changed dramatically by the time of the Civil War. A variety of factors combined to fuel a runaway expansion of the economy. Poor transportation facilities, the dearth of capital for investment, and chronic labor shortages had inhibited growth in the early national period. After 1815 improvements in existing land routes and the construction first of canals and then of railroads sharply reduced transport costs and led to the emergence of a national market. Income from exports, particularly cotton and grains, helped to finance these developments, while the proliferation of state banks made credit and money more generally available. Bank notes became "the major circulating medium" of the market revolution.[3] Population increase was another important stimulant to the economy. The high native birthrate and the influx of immigrants in the second quarter of the century "provided an elastic supply of labor conducive to manufacturing growth."[4] Cities expanded even faster than the population of the country as a whole, ensuring large concentrated markets for foodstuffs and consumer goods. Statistics convey some sense of the magnitude of these changes: between 1820 and 1860 the population grew from about 10 million to almost 32 million while the proportion of Americans dwelling in cities rose by 800 percent; railroad mileage went from zero to over thirty thousand; and there was a fivefold increase in the number of banks and the value of notes in circulation.[5]

The remarkable pace of economic growth doomed the family-based structures of the household regime. A rising percentage of the nation's resources and productive capacities was directed toward the market, and gain rather than self-sufficiency became the driving motive for many Americans. Cash-crop agriculture, encouraged by the size and accessibility of urban markets as well as by the invention of more efficient implements, gradually replaced subsistence farming. The rise of manufacturing establishments accelerated the movement away from domestic industry and destroyed the apprenticeship system. By mid-century finished products formerly made in the household were being turned out in workshops and factories owned by entrepreneurs. References to home-spun cloth were once common in New England account books and family records; after 1830 they decline and virtually disappear.[6] Goods were increasingly machine produced, and growing numbers of men and women sold their labor on the open market instead of working in the home. Although only about 4 percent of the American work force was employed in factories on the eve of the Civil War, areas of the Northeast were as heavily industrialized as the manufacturing regions of Great Britain. A national economy was in place, and the United States ranked second among the leading commercial and industrial nations of the world.[7]

Writing and publishing developed along roughly the same lines as the economy at large: prior to 1820 they had not yet assumed their modern character as professional undertakings. Books were expensive to manufacture and difficult to distribute widely. Although the system of patronage had never taken root in America, belles-lettres had remained an upper-class or patrician pursuit. Shared interests and knowledge often connected the author and his limited audience. Moreover, writers enjoyed a certain control over their work because they usually hired publishers and paid them a percentage of the profits. Publishers themselves had little incentive to encourage native literature. In the absence of international copyright laws, they were naturally more inclined to reprint foreign books on which they had no obligation to share the profits. Only the rare American work could sell enough copies to surmount this handicap and become a paying proposition.[8]

During the next three decades sweeping changes occurred in the production, circulation, and status of literature. Technological advancements like the cylinder press vastly speeded up the printing process by mechanizing operations that had previously been performed by hand. With the innovation of cloth bindings and improved ways of making paper, it was now possible to produce books in larger editions and at lower prices than ever before. Railroads removed many of the obstacles to distribution, linking up the different regions of the country and providing eastern publishers with access to the interior. As a result of population growth and enhanced opportunities for education, the audience for literature was not only more truly national but also substantially increased in size. By 1850, when over 90 percent of adult whites could read and write, the United States boasted the largest literate public in history.⁹ A mass market existed for books, and aggressive, highly competitive publishing houses emerged to meet the demand. The new firms took charge of all details of the business, and authors lost most of their earlier control over publication. But authors also gained from these developments: the appearance of a mass readership meant that publishers could realistically expect to make a profit on books written by Americans. From 1820 to 1830 Americans published 109 fictional works by their countrymen; in the 1840s this number jumped to almost a thousand. The value of books of all categories manufactured and sold here reached $12.5 million by the end of the decade, five times more than in 1820. Publishing had become an industry, and the writer a producer of commodities for the literary marketplace.¹⁰

There was no stronger indication of the commercializing of letters than the new importance paid to advertising. An audience of distant consumers required assiduous cultivation if an author was to achieve significant sales; common concerns and allegiances could no longer be taken for granted. Cultural entrepreneurs devised sophisticated techniques for merchandising art, treating the writer's biography and even his appearance as important factors in the selling of his books. In the 1820s privacy was still possible for the man of letters. Hawthorne could embark on a literary career by retiring to a room in his mother's house and serving a self-imposed apprenticeship of a dozen years. Thirty years later Melville refused his portrait to the magazines because this particular form of puffery had become so commonplace, as he wrote to a friend, that the "test of distinction is getting to be reversed; and, therefore, to see one's 'mug' in a magazine, is presumptive evidence that he's a nobody."¹¹

American civilization and art, in short, were radically and permanently altered as a result of the spread of a market economy. When I speak of market society, I refer to a set of relations that characterized a particular phase in the evolution of capitalism. People and their surroundings were brought under the dominion of exchange, and all transactions, including those between the author and his readers, were turned into money transactions. Encompassing commercialization and, to a lesser extent, industrialization, the market order can be distinguished from both the self-sufficient orientation of the eighteenth century and the system of large-scale corporations predominant after the Civil War.

No one aspect of the "Great Transformation," as this historical moment has been called,[12] monopolized the attention of the romantic artists. While I have tried to respect the complexity and diversity of the romantic response, I make no claims to comprehensiveness. This is a study of limited scope, a series of essays on a common topic, and I have not hesitated to be selective in my choice of authors. I have singled out for examination four figures whose work is undeniably major: Emerson, Thoreau, Hawthorne, and Melville. Although my focus is on the literature and not on societal change, a broad historical progression has emerged, a movement from the collapse of the agrarian ideal in Emerson and Thoreau, through the commercializing of culture affecting Hawthorne and Melville, to the problem of class stratification in "Bartleby, the Scrivener."

I have taken my cue from the writers themselves in emphasizing those features of the new regime which they addressed in their art. To the early Emerson, the spread of the market meant instability and the loss of independence; the later Emerson found order and reassurance in the same circumstances from which his younger self recoiled. To Thoreau, capitalist growth brought with it the disfigurement of nature, alienation from one's labor, and a pervasive feeling that men no longer controlled their own lives. Hawthorne, who was primarily concerned with the market's impact on the writer, returned time and again to the necessity for wooing customers and making a positive impression on the public. Melville grappled with the vanishing of the human in the commodity form, a phenomenon as relevant for literary artifacts as for the objects of the physical world. He also wrote about the deepening of class divisions that accompanied the transition from a household to a rationalized economy. The chapters on Melville contain an implicit argument that the market develops historically from its manifestation in commodities to its role in fostering the social segregation of classes.

Most interpretations of the romantic writers see them as oppositional in their attitude toward the values and social consequences of the market revolution. All have been portrayed as unreservedly hostile to the emergent order's rationalistic, calculating outlook, its uprooting of traditional structures, and its relentless monetizing of human relations. Leo Marx, in his study of American pastoralism, has emphasized the antitechnocratic side of the romantic movement, showing how the classic nineteenth-century texts express resistance to the onset of industrialization. Other scholars have explored the romantic dissatisfaction with the subjection of art to the rule of the market. Henry Nash Smith, for example, argues that Hawthorne and Melville repudiated the ideology of popular culture and deliberately affronted the expectations of their readers. Smith contrasts the two novelists to the sentimental women writers who catered to middle-brow tastes and were rewarded with commercial success. William Charvat and Ann Douglas view Melville in particular as chafing at his dependency on a public whose values and judgment he despised.[13]

Ample evidence exists to support this conception of American romanticism as a movement of dissent. Emerson's essays abound in attacks on materialism and on the social inequities fostered by the market system. "Let there be worse cotton and better men," he declares in protesting the degradation of the laboring classes in New England's rapidly growing mills. Emerson regarded conformity, his special bugbear, as a problem not of Society in the abstract but of the particular social environment emerging under capitalism. Business culture was anathema to self-reliance because it placed so much importance on how one appeared to others: "We foolishly think, in our days of sin, that we must court friends by compliance to the customs of society, to its dress, its breeding and its estimates."[14] Thoreau took up many of the same themes in launching his own attacks on "the commercial spirit of modern times." In *Walden* he condemns the factory system for impoverishing the operatives to enrich the corporations, and he advises his readers to "beware of all enterprises that require new clothes."[15]

Each of the four writers considered here objected to the reduction of literature to the status of a commodity; each expressed resentment at the reading public whose preferences governed the market. Hawthorne, in his well-known diatribe against the "scribbling women," voiced a typical judgment on the value of popularity: "I should have no chance of success while the public taste is occupied with their trash—and should be ashamed of myself if I did succeed." According to Thoreau, the ways of earning money "almost without exception lead downward. . . . If you would get money as a writer or lecturer, you must be popular, which is to go down perpendicularly." A distinction was often drawn between the vulgar mass and a more discriminating audience. Emerson differentiated between the "partial and noisy readers of the hour," whose verdicts set the fashion, and "an eternal public" capable of appreciating genius, "a public not to be bribed, not to be entreated, and not to be overawed." For Melville, the crucial division was between the enlightened "people" and the imperceptive "public," the latter being a monster "with the head of a jackass, the body of a baboon, and the tail of a scorpion." [16]

The split between elite and mass culture registered in these remarks appears to be confirmed by the actual literary market. While the romantics were producing the masterpieces still read today, domestic novels written by women commanded the enthusiasm of the antebellum public. In the decade before the Civil War, a succession of unprecedented bestsellers overwhelmed the American publishing scene. At a time when Hawthorne could hope to appeal to five or perhaps six thousand readers, a first novel by one of the female authors, Susan B. Warner's *The Wide, Wide World* (1850), amazed and delighted its publishers by selling over forty thousand copies in less than a year. The book went into its fourteenth printing by 1852 and eventually attracted more than a million buyers. Comparable levels of popularity were attained by "Fanny Fern" (the pen name of Sara Parton), Mary Virginia Terhune, E. D. E. N. Southworth, Maria Cummins, and other women novelists. *The Lamplighter* (1854), Cummins's first book, recorded forty thousand in sales after only eight weeks and exceeded seventy thousand by the end of a year. [17]

If the "feminine fifties," as this decade has been called, represented a triumph of the mass market, the celebration was not one in which the romantic artists shared. The same years saw the publication of some of the canonical works of American literature, including *The Scarlet Letter* (1850), *Representative Men* (1850), *Moby-Dick* (1851), *The House of the Seven Gables* (1851), *Pierre* (1852), and *Walden* (1854); but most of these books sold poorly, and none achieved more than a modest success. "All of them together probably did not in that decade add up to the sales of one of the more popular domestic novels." [18] Though Hawthorne had a larger following than the other romantics, his income from writing remained pitifully small compared to the financial gains being reaped by more commercial authors. The stark difference was brought home to him in 1853 by G. P. Putnam, the publisher of his volume of tales, *Mosses from an Old Manse*, as well as of Warner's *Wide, Wide World*. Having calculated Hawthorne's royalties for the past year and a half at $144.09, Putnam wrote to explain that "the last two semi-annual accounts were passed over by our bookkeeper simply because the amount was small." The publishing firm itself was not to blame for these disappointing figures, Putnam added, gratuitously pointing out that Warner's novel had earned its author $4,500 in the most recent six-month period. [19] Given such disparities, the romantics can be excused for feeling that they inhabited a completely separate cultural universe from the "scribbling women." They had reason to excoriate a literary market that proved so inhospitable to their art.

Criticism of the market regime was not confined to a handful of major writers; many people in the mid-nineteenth century felt uneasy about the dislocations caused by modernization. The Age of Jackson was an era of acute conflict about the advantages and drawbacks of capitalist development. Although the Great Transformation improved the living conditions of most Americans, it also brought social upheaval and threatened the economic independence of large segments of the population. Struggles were joined between those who gained from the expanding market and those who were injured by it, between rising merchants and manufacturers on the one hand and declining farmers and unskilled laborers on the other. There were also struggles within individual men and women who both applauded and feared the forces of change. Even persons who welcomed economic progress, with its increased prospects for social mobility, its higher standard of living, and its technological conveniences, experienced anxiety and forboding about the direction of the nation. In an age of unprecedented growth, they looked wistfully toward the stable agrarian order of the past, torn between the old republican virtues and the acquisitive ethos of a society based on the pursuit of self-interest.[20]

My contention is that the four authors in this study shared their culture's ambivalent reaction to the extension of the market. While they were harshly critical of the new economic order, they were also strongly drawn to what they saw as the positive effects of commerce, and they were all willing, at least for a time, to accommodate themselves to the imperatives of writing for the mass public. They fought out in their careers and art the question of the market's merits and liabilities. Emerson went from condemnation to celebration of the modern economy, and even in his agrarian phase he had praise for industrialists and merchant-capitalists as men of strong will who imposed their designs on nature. He had a lifelong fascination with what might be called the moral economy of capitalism, regularly discovering lessons for the spirit in the procedures of the countinghouse. "This Book is my Savings Bank," he wrote in his journal not long after leaving the pulpit. "I grow richer because I have somewhere to deposit my earnings; and fractions are worth more to me because corresponding fractions are waiting that shall be made integers by their addition." Even in a book as hostile to exchange as *Walden*, one is startled to find passages full of admiration for commercial enterprise. Inspired by the sound of the railroad passing near his cabin, Thoreau enthuses over trade as "unexpectedly confident and serene, alert, adventurous, and unwearied." Melville's experience as a common sailor exposed him to the interdependence of working men under the division of labor and convinced him of the power of commerce to break down local prejudices and build trust among different nationalities. In *Redburn* he writes of a dock at Liverpool:

> Here are brought together the remotest limits of the earth; and in the collective spars and timbers of these ships, all the forests of the globe are represented, as in a grand parliament of masts. Canada and New Zealand send their pines; America her live oak; India her teak; Norway her spruce; and the Right Honorable Mahogany, member for Honduras and Campeachy, is seen at his post by the wheel. Here, under the beneficent sway of the Genius of Commerce, all climes and countries embrace; and yard-arm touches yard-arm in brotherly love.[21]

The tension or doubleness in the romantics' response to the marketplace can also be seen in their equivocal feelings about popularity. Emerson falls into a somewhat different category from the other three because financial security insulated him from the need to sell; yet his disdain for the "noisy readers of the hour" did not prevent him from hoping to appeal to both audiences, the many as well as the select few. In his funeral oration for Thoreau, he relates a dialogue with his fellow Concordian in which Thoreau is quoted as saying "that whatever succeeded with the audience was bad." Emerson's rejoinder reveals a disposition on his own part to please the public: "Who would not like to write something which all can read, like Robinson Crusoe? and who does not see with regret that his page is not solid with a right materialistic treatment, which delights everybody?"[22]

Thoreau rather than his mentor emerges from this exchange as the quintessential disaffected romantic: he objected vigorously to Emerson's attitude and "vaunted the better lectures which reached only a few persons."[23] Yet while Thoreau was unquestionably the least conciliatory of the four writers, it is an error to see him as a pure "nonprofessional" holding himself serenely aloof from the business end of literature. He had far more interest in popular success than has commonly been supposed. Although he refused to make concessions to public taste (unlike Hawthorne and Melville), he wanted to influence the thinking of his countrymen and to reach as many people as possible through his lectures and writing. Moreover, he was in constant need of money. Emerson himself had a clear sense of his young friend's desires when Thoreau was seeking a publisher for *A Week on the Concord and Merrimack Rivers*. He stated in a letter of 1847, "Thoreau is mainly bent on having it printed in a cheap form for a large circulation."[24] Thoreau's concern with the trade of authorship dominated his correspondence with Horace Greeley, the shrewd New York editor who acted for several years as his informal literary agent. Their letters are filled with monetary details and accounts of negotiations with publishers, and Thoreau was willing to follow Greeley's advice about how to promote himself with the reading public. "You may write with an angel's pen, yet your writings have no mercantile, money value till you are known and talked of as an author," wrote Greeley in a typical passage. He urged Thoreau to advertise his works by publishing chapters in advance, and Thoreau obliged by printing excerpts from *Walden* in newspapers and magazines to drum up interest in the book.[25]

Melville and Hawthorne depended on book sales for their livelihood, and their dismissals of popularity should be weighed against their financial exigencies as well as their commitment to democracy. Melville's dubious distinction between "the public" and "the people" indicates the nature of his dilemma: he vowed "to hate the one and cleave to the other," yet in a democratic society who else constitutes the hated public but precisely the beloved people, the mass of ordinary readers?[26] Melville told his English publisher that his first book, *Typee*, was "calculated for popular reading, or for none at all," and he expressed readiness to excise passages which "offer violence to the feelings of any large class of readers." He himself initiated the proposal for issuing a revised English edition, assuring the publisher "that it will be policy so to do."[27] The "gentle Hawthorne," as he was known in the nineteenth century, could be equally hard-headed in scheming with his publisher. When Ticknor and Fields tried to capitalize on the success of *The Scarlet Letter* by bringing out new editions of his previous works, he discouraged them from reprinting *Fanshawe*, his own first novel, on the grounds that it would impair his marketability: "Whatever might do me credit you may be pretty sure I should be ready enough to bring forward. Anything else it is our mutual interest to conceal."[28]

The marketplace, then, was a contested issue for the American romantics, a source not of simple opposition but of complex and often contradictory attitudes. Their major works are deeply marked by their divided feelings about the changes transforming their roles as writers and revolutionizing their society. These tensions can be traced in structure as well as in theme: the formal dissonances of *Moby-Dick* and *The Scarlet Letter*, for example, grew out of their authors' indecision about their identity as producers of literary commodities and about their relation to the mass reading public which they wished to cultivate quite as much as they resented. The greatness of the two novels demonstrates that the conflicts aroused by the new conditions could be beneficial to literature, and sometimes in ways that the writer himself did not intend. *Walden* is an example of a book that was changed for the better as a consequence of the economics of publication in antebellum America. But if the marketplace could work to the advantage of some texts, it could also produce deformity in others, and I argue that Hawthorne's wish to give the public what he believed they wanted led to the flawed conclusion of *The House of the Seven Gables*.

The presence of contradictions in American romantic art has of course been noticed before; as early as the 1830s, Alexis de Tocqueville surmised that democratic literature would be defined by its polarities. In the twentieth century, the idea has been associated primarily with Richard Chase, who developed Tocqueville's hints into a seminal thesis about the American romance as a genre of irreconcilable opposites. Chase proposed several explanations for the dualism of the American imagination, among them the weakness of mediating institutions in the nineteenth century and the Manichean sensibility bred by Puritanism.[29] I would supplement Chase's argument by pointing to the growth of the exchange economy as one of the underlying causes of the tensions of American romanticism.

Moreover, I believe that many of the conflicts troubling Hawthorne and Melville in particular, as novelists in search of a national audience, were shared by other writers of the period from 1820 to 1860. As stated earlier, my concern in this study has been illustrative rather than exhaustive; I have not tried to investigate every important romantic artist who went through the experience of professionalization. Yet I hope that this book illuminates critical aspects of the process and that certain of my findings will prove relevant for authors not considered here. Irving and Cooper, as members of a slightly older generation, and Poe, as a contemporary, also had to deal with the problem of writing for the mass public. One would expect to discover that dependency on the market inspired them with a similar mixture of accommodation and resistance.

Ambivalence toward the exchange process also links the romantics to more popular authors, such as the literary women, who are ordinarily perceived as their opposites. The rift between high and middlebrow culture, of which the romantics themselves complained, needs to be qualified by the recognition that they too were interested in selling. Furthermore, recent scholarship has challenged the picture of the domestic novelists as unthinking conformists with no misgivings about consumer culture. It appears that the women's reactions to the literary marketplace were far more complicated than has usually been supposed. What caused them special anguish was their singular position as celebrants of private domestic life who occupied the public stage as best-selling authors.[30] Hawthorne, who was most contemptuous of the female novelists, was also most like them: no conflict disturbed him more than that between his longing for popularity and his dread of having his inner being violated. Hawthorne even confessed his admiration for the women in a moment of candor and contrition. "I bestowed some vituperation on female authors. I have since been reading 'Ruth Hall' [a novel by Fanny Fern]; and I must say I enjoyed it a good deal. The woman writes as if the Devil was in her; and that is the only condition under which a woman ever writes anything worth reading." This is high praise indeed from the author who described his own book, *The Scarlet Letter*, as "positively a hell-fired story."[31]

Thus far, in tracing the romantic writers' contradictory responses to the market, I have emphasized that they were highly alert to and articulate about the emergent order's implications. But they were also products of history, men shaped in spite of themselves by the times in which they lived; the Great Transformation had effects on their thinking of which they were unconscious or only fitfully aware. In other words, there are affinities between romanticism and the marketplace that go beyond the question of a given author's contempt for popularity or desire for success. Paradoxically, these underlying connections often seem inextricable from attempts to repudiate commercial society altogether. Traits of romantic art that arise out of antagonism toward the market system prove upon closer inspection to replicate the very conditions against which they protest. Even on this more latent level, the relationship between literature and economic change is neither wholly disabling nor empowering but a complex combination of the two.

Certainly in one sense the romantics can be seen as casualties of the new developments. The market imposed limits on the possibilities available to them as writers in the mid-nineteenth century, limits that defeated their hopes for certain kinds of authority or for closeness to their readers. Authorial ambitions and aesthetic programs were rendered obsolete by the same social and economic revolution that overtook subsistence farming and replaced hand-made items with manufactured products. But it was precisely because of the thwarting of such hopes that the classic nineteenth-century works acquired their distinctive qualities. Disappointment impelled the romantics toward textual strategies of difficulty and concealment, causing them to reconstruct in their relations to their audience the alienation they criticized in modern society. I examine several of these double-sided interactions in the following chapters and would like to sketch out here two illustrations of how the marketplace determined the character and development of American romanticism. The first has to do with Thoreau's frustrated aspiration to exert influence in the political realm. The second concerns the relation between symbolism and the commodity form and helps to explain the disillusionment with fiction that overcame both Hawthorne and Melville.

Emerson was perhaps the first to complain of unrealized potential in his disciple—potential not as a writer but as a man of action. In the memorial address, he is unable to suppress his disappointment that Thoreau did not apply his considerable talents to the betterment of society:

> Had his genius been only contemplative, he had been fitted to his life, but with his energy and practical ability he seemed born for great enterprise and for command; and I so much regret the loss of his rare powers of action, that I cannot help counting it a fault in him that he had no ambition. Wanting this, instead of engineering for all America, he was the captain of a huckleberry-party. Pounding beans is good to the end of pounding empires one of these days; but if, at the end of years, it is still only beans!

Emerson is thinking here of the experiment at Walden and of the night Thoreau spent in jail for refusing to pay his poll tax, the morning after which he took charge of a huckleberry party, as he reports in "Civil Disobedience."[32]

There is no question that Thoreau had a very different conception of his purpose. From the beginning of his literary career, he was interested in achieving authority over his fellow men. An apprentice piece, written while he was still an undergraduate at Harvard, deals with "the Methods of gaining and exercising public Influence." Later works explicitly identify this ambition with the calling of the writer. In his essay on Thomas Carlyle, Thoreau praises the Scotchman as an example of "the hero, as literary man," and in *A Week* he defines the unity of heroism and literature he admires and seeks to embody in himself. The poet, he claims, once combined the offices of hero and bard and was as capable of doing combat as the warriors whom he encouraged with his lays. "But now," Thoreau laments, "the hero and the bard are of different professions." The poet "only conceives the deed, which he formerly stood ready to perform." Thoreau proposes to reunify the two vocations by having the literary man act for himself, as he did in resisting the government, but more importantly by integrating speech and action. He believes that literature should have the force and impact of physical deeds; it should not merely chronicle or reflect events but bring them to pass by inspiring men to act. The author should be "a Cincinnatus in literature," a leader who uses the pen to galvanize his reader-followers and "make [them] dangerous to existing institutions."[33]

Thoreau wrote "Civil Disobedience" and began *Walden* with the intention of fulfilling this last objective. Both works aspire to public influence, and both specify the hero-bard as a kind of transcendent legislator who discerns the truth with special clarity because of his position of detachment. In the essay, Thoreau reproves contemporary lawmakers for failing to "speak with authority" on the urgent issues of the day. They stand "so completely within the institution" that they "never distinctly and nakedly behold it. They speak of moving society, but have no resting-place without it."[34] On July fourth, a day all Americans associate with revolution, Thoreau retired to Walden Pond in search of such a "resting-place," a critical vantage point where he could write the texts that would arouse his countrymen to renovate the nation. His goal in going to the woods, he suggests in *Walden*, is to enroll himself among "the benefactors of the race, whom we have apotheosized as messengers from heaven, bearers of divine gifts to man."[35]

Yet one is struck in reading the book by what seems (and seemed

to Thoreau's contemporaries) a discrepancy in tone and content between the opening treatment of "Economy" and the final chapters.
There is a perceptible movement away from the social world and
from the hope of inaugurating civic change through literature. At
some point in the process of composition Thoreau appears to have
forsaken his political ambitions in order to produce a lapidary masterpiece of private consciousness. I suggest in Chapter 2 that the marketplace was indirectly responsible for this shift in purpose. Because
Thoreau deplored the effects of commerce on literature, he tried to
find some way to overcome the commodifying of his text. In doing
so, he adopted techniques that would forestall easy consumption of
what he wrote. When the public showed little interest in the heroic
reading he demanded, he was forced to amend his expectations as a
poet-legislator. Thoreau settled for the captaincy of a huckleberry
party—and for the writing of an intricate classic—but it was not so
much lack of ambition, as Emerson supposed, as it was the "curse of
trade" that lay behind his retreat from the possibility of "engineering
for all America."

Trade also seems to be connected to the appearance of symbolism
in the writings of the American romantics. It is a fact of literary history that the flourishing of the symbolistic method in this country,
whatever its possible antecedents in Puritanism, coincided with the
expansion of the capitalist marketplace. In my discussions of Emerson and Thoreau, I outline a way of relating the symbolic mentality
to the developments in the economy, specifically to the spread of the
commodity form. As more and more of the physical world falls under
the domination of the market, objects increasingly assume a kind of
doubleness. They exist in their own right, as material objects, but as
commodities they come to possess a second significance or function,
as bearers of value. They can be used or consumed, and they can be
exchanged for money.[36] The twofold nature of things is a growing
economic phenomenon that finds its correlative in the symbolic
mode of apprehension. The symbolist also perceives the world as
twofold: things have a concrete reality for him, and at the same time
they signify an idea or another object. They are "exchangeable" for
something else. In my chapter on Emerson, I point out that the little
book entitled *Nature*, which contains his principal exposition of the
symbolic method, begins with a section on "Commodity": the Emersonian way of looking at the world suggests the influence of the
market system upon consciousness. I believe that Thoreau recog-
nized this point, and in my analysis of *Walden* I indicate how he tries

(and ultimately fails) to free his own mind and art from the abstraction of the commodity form.

The Marxist critic Georg Lukács has proposed a different way of accounting for the relation between symbolic thinking and the transformation of the economy. For Lukács, symbolism arises as a response not to doubleness but to absence; the symbolist creates meaning where none otherwise exists. Symbolism, he argues, becomes a dominant quality in literary works only after capitalism has reached a relatively "finished" stage of evolution. In modern industrial civilization, objects are no longer produced by hand and their link to human labor is concealed. These commodified objects appear to lead an independent existence. In contemplating them, the writer can find no trace of their human origin, and he is compelled to construct a fictive meaning to compensate for the apparent emptiness or muteness of his surroundings. Symbolism is the effort of the literary imagination to impose significance upon the world of things from which capitalist production has banished the human element.[37]

Lukács advanced his interpretation of symbolism in discussions of modern European literature, and there are difficulties in trying to apply his argument to the antebellum American situation. As I have emphasized, the Jacksonian era was a transitional time in the development of capitalism. While the commodity form was becoming more pervasive, its triumph was not yet complete; the connection between things and man's labor had not wholly been effaced. There was still resistance to the new order, and some objects were still being produced by hand under the old artisanal or household arrangements. In literature, too, there was resistance to the dehumanization of the commodity form. Books were now articles of trade, to be sure, but authors like Thoreau, Hawthorne, and Melville sought to combat the effects of commercialization on their writing. Melville, who was himself a symbolist, even criticized the symbolic habit of thought on the very grounds that Lukács did. In *Moby-Dick* he implies that the crucial point of resemblance between the commodity and the symbol is the erasure of the human in both. He faults Ahab for reading significance into the objects of the world without acknowledging his own complicity in the attribution of meaning to nature. The Captain reproduces in the realm of thought the same mystification of human agency that the capitalist market fosters in the economic sphere.

Lukács's analysis seems more relevant to certain American works written after the Civil War: notably Frank Norris's *McTeague*, where the symbols put in by the author—the gold tooth, the canary in a cage, and so on—are arbitrary and contrived. By 1899, when *Mc-Teague* was published, the social and economic conditions described by Lukács had long since been established in the United States. Indeed, they were largely predominant by 1860, the agrarian and household structures of the past having been steadily eclipsed by the growth of the market. That the Age of Jackson was a time of transition should not obscure the fact that the extension of the commodity form over man and nature proceeded inexorably throughout the period. The commodity form also solidified its hold on literature: the storyteller and his audience confronted each other solely in the capacity of a seller of goods and potential customers. The consequences of this historical reality can be traced in the thwarted efforts of a Hawthorne or a Melville to resist the alienation of the artwork. As I demonstrate in my chapters on the two fiction writers, they attempted to forge some kind of human bond with their readers: to deny or circumvent the impersonal relation of exchange. Melville's companionable first-person narrators, appealing to a circle of fraternal listeners; Hawthorne's dreams of encountering "the one heart and mind of perfect sympathy"[38]—these essentially artisanal versions of author-audience relations were fated to be disappointed. Obliged to undertake impersonal market calculations to survive economically, the two novelists eventually succumbed to the commodifying process. They came to see their readers as adversaries and their books as alienated objects. Especially in the later fictions of Melville, the link between the text and its human maker has virtually disappeared. The disavowal of man's activity that for Lukács defined both the symbol and the commodity becomes, in an elusive fiction like *The Confidence-Man*, the hallmark of the entire literary work.

1

Emerson and the Persistence
of the Commodity

In Emerson's essay "Wealth" there appears a glowing account of peaches destined for the market: "When the farmer's peaches are taken from under the tree and carried into town, they have a new look and a hundredfold value over the fruit which grew on the same bough and lies fulsomely on the ground. The craft of the merchant is this bringing a thing from where it abounds to where it is costly."[1]

It is instructive to compare this passage with the one in *Walden* where Thoreau condemns the marketing of huckleberries: "The fruits do not yield their true flavor to the purchaser of them, nor to him who raises them for market. . . . It is a vulgar error to suppose that you have tasted huckleberries who never plucked them. A huckleberry never reaches Boston; they have not been known there since they grew on her three hills. The ambrosial and essential part of the fruit is lost with the bloom which is rubbed off in the market cart, and they become mere provender. As long as Eternal Justice reigns, not one innocent huckleberry can be transported thither from the country's hills."[2]

For Emerson, the transformation of nature's fruits into commodities gives them "a new look" and multiplies their value "a hundredfold"; for Thoreau, the identical process empties the world of significance, draining the huckleberry of its "true flavor" and "essential

This chapter originally appeared under the same title in *Emerson: Prospect and Retrospect*, ed. Joel Porte, Harvard English Studies, vol. 10 (Cambridge, Mass.: Harvard University Press, 1982), pp. 65–84. Reprinted by permission of Harvard University Press.

part." Though "Wealth" was not published until 1860, Emerson first delivered it in lecture form as early as 1851–52, when Thoreau was working on his revisions of *Walden*; the two passages might almost have been written as rebuttals to each other. Indeed, the sentiments of "Wealth" seem to constitute a rebuttal not only to Thoreau's economic views but to those expressed by Emerson himself before his drift toward conservatism. In earlier writings Emerson is less "the seer of *laisser-faire* capitalism," in Daniel Aaron's phrase,[3] than a critic of the marketplace for whom nature, regarded solely as commodity, "is debased, as if one looking at the ocean can remember only the price of fish."[4] This Emerson takes his ideal of self-reliance from the agrarian or Jeffersonian past rather than the commercial and industrial future. In common with many of his contemporaries, he sees the new economic order as a threat to individual autonomy, an indication not so much of man's power over his environment as of the instability of the material world. Yet even at this stage of his career one can detect the Emerson who will subsequently assert in "Wealth," "The counting-room maxims liberally expounded are laws of the universe. The merchant's economy is a coarse symbol of the soul's economy" (*W* 6:125). These contradictions and inconsistencies in his attitude toward the market regime are precisely what locate Emerson in the history of his period and make him a truly "representative man" of Jacksonian America.[5]

The antimarket side of Emerson is most prominent in works dating from the depression of 1837–43. In "The Transcendentalist," a lecture of 1841, he himself characterizes the "new views" prevalent in New England as a reaction against the commercialism of the age. "What is popularly called Transcendentalism among us," he notes, "is Idealism; Idealism as it appears in 1842" (*CW* 1:201). In other epochs the hunger for spiritual truth made patriots or protestants; the same impulse, "falling on Unitarian and commercial times, makes the peculiar shades of Idealism which we know" (*CW* 1:206). Although Emerson is not an uncritical admirer of the disaffected youth who adopt the Transcendental philosophy, he does share their objections to "the common labors and competitions of the market" (*CW* 1:207).

"Man the Reformer," another lecture of 1841, is outspoken in attacking the modern capitalist economy and enumerating the "sins" habitual in exchange. "The general system of our trade," Emerson declares, ". . . is a system of selfishness . . . of distrust, of concealment, of superior keenness, not of giving but of taking advantage." He is careful to point out that the abuses of commerce are not confined to the merchant or manufacturer. The farmer who raises crops for market is also implicated, as is the consumer: "it is only necessary to ask a few questions as to the progress of the articles of commerce from the fields where they grew, to our houses, to become aware that we eat and drink and wear perjury and fraud in a hundred commodities" (*CW* 1:147–48). Government, education, and even religion have been infected by the mercantile spirit, Emerson says elsewhere in assessing "the present age." And he concludes, "There is nothing more important in the culture of man than to resist the dangers of commerce."[6]

Emerson's dislike of "commercial times" is closely bound up with his individualism; self-reliance, in his view, is not a corollary but a casualty of exchange relations. Nonconformity cannot survive the interactions of the marketplace, where the requirements for success include "a certain dapperness and compliance, an acceptance of customs . . . a compromise of private opinion and lofty integrity." Every man is constrained to put on "the harness of routine and obsequiousness" in order to earn money (*CW* 1:147–48). In the essay "Self-Reliance" (1841), Emerson uses an image drawn from commerce to convey his sense that capitalist society extinguishes independence: "Society is a joint-stock company in which the members agree for the better securing of his bread to each shareholder, to surrender the liberty and culture of the eater" (*CW* 2:29).

The young Transcendentalist withdraws into idleness to avoid this condition. Even reform holds limited appeal for him because movements like Temperance or Abolition tend to degenerate into marketable commodities and to lose their integrity in the process of exchange. Each cause, Emerson explains, "becomes speedily a little shop, where the article, let it have been at first never so subtle and ethereal, is now made up into portable and convenient cakes, and retailed in small quantities to suit purchasers" (*CW* 1:211). To the Transcendentalist, who above all cherishes his autonomy, any activity is distasteful that requires courting others. "It is simpler to be self-dependent," he believes. "The height, the deity of man is to be self-sustained, to need no gift, no foreign force" (*CW* 1:203–4).

Admittedly, the Transcendentalist has as yet produced "no solid fruit" in his isolation (*CW* 1:207). He is nevertheless a recognizable if somewhat Hamlet-like descendant of the Jeffersonian husbandman. According to Jefferson, the hallmark of the cultivator is his abstention from exchange. His virtue is secure because he relies for his livelihood on "his own soil and industry" and does not "depend for it on the casualties and caprice of customers."[7] For Emerson, the husbandman's example is the antidote to "the ways of trade." As he observes in "Man the Reformer," there seems no escape from the compromises and dependencies of commerce save "to begin the world anew, as he does who puts the spade into the ground for food" (*CW* 1:147).

Emerson is far from insisting that everyone should become a farmer. What he holds up for imitation is not the actual practice of husbandry but the principle of self-sufficiency contained in "the doctrine of the Farm," the doctrine "that every man ought to stand in primary relations with the work of the world, ought to do it himself" (*CW* 1:152, 155). This program, which Thoreau was to carry out at Walden Pond, essentially involves reducing one's wants and endeavoring to satisfy them oneself so as to minimize dependence on others. It demands intellectual independence as well as plain living and points to the affirmations of "Self-Reliance," where Emerson again employs a metaphor, this time drawn from farming, to illustrate his idea of self-trust: "There is a time in every man's education when he arrives at the conviction that envy is ignorance; that imitation is suicide; that he must take himself for better, for worse, as his portion; that though the wide universe is full of good, no kernel of nourishing corn can come to him but through his toil bestowed on that plot of ground which is given to him to till" (*CW* 2:27–28).

Emerson's affirmation of agrarian values indicates how close he is in some respects to his Jacksonian contemporaries. As Marvin Meyers has shown, the Jacksonians considered themselves heirs to the Jeffersonian tradition; they appealed to the yeoman ideals of the Old Republic in their war against the Bank of the United States, the institution that symbolized for them the emergent capitalist economy. Despite their pronouncements in favor of laissez faire, they were beset by fears of a world out of control; the actual workings of the market seemed incoherent to them rather than rational and orderly. Jackson himself, in denouncing the banking system as a threat to economic independence, repeatedly used language expressive of randomness and chaotic change: "great and sudden fluctuations . . . rendering property insecure and the wages of labor unsteady and uncertain," "unexpected and ruinous contraction," "ebbs and flows in the currency." Meyers notes the epistemological strain in these attacks on the "Monster Bank," which flooded the economy with paper money "having of itself no intrinsic value," in Jackson's words. Since the Jacksonians linked freedom to economic self-reliance, to "tangibles owned and controlled," as Meyers puts it, and ultimately to the land, the survival of liberty itself, they believed, depended on their struggle to check the growth of capitalism.[8]

Emerson draws near to this fearful side of Jacksonianism in a journal entry for 1838: "This invasion of Nature by Trade with its Money, its Steam, its Railroad, threatens to upset the balance of man, and establish a new Universal Monarchy more tyrannical than Babylon or Rome."[9] His sense that nature has been violated by commerce was widely shared at this time in America, where, as he remarked in 1844, "out of doors all seems a market" (*CW* 1:239). As the United States transformed itself from a static, agrarian economy to a mobile, commercial society, land itself was drawn into the orbit of the market and was dethroned "from the supreme position it had occupied in the eighteenth-century world view." It was now perceived as an asset to be developed for profit or an object of speculation, liable, like any commodity, to arbitrary and fluctuating assessments of its value. Under the market regime, value itself came to be regarded as subjective, determined not by the inherent properties of an object but by extrinsic factors such as opinion and desire. Clearly it was not only paper money that seemed to have "of itself no intrinsic value" in Jackson's America. Indeed, the Jacksonian campaign against the Bank can be seen as merely the surface expression of a deeper uneasiness over what Karl Polanyi has called "the extreme artificiality of market economy." To convert land and labor into articles of exchange, Polanyi points out, is to make them into "fictitious" commodities, to treat them according to the falsehood that they are produced for sale on the market. It is to allow the process of exchange to set a price on human beings and their natural surroundings.[10] Or as Emerson himself observes, trade "goes to put everything *into market*, talent, beauty, virtue, and man himself" (*CW* 1:234). In "The Transcendentalist," it will be recalled, Emerson claims that "commercial times" give rise to Idealism; what lies behind this, he suggests in "Man the Reformer," is dissatisfaction with the artificial valuations of market culture: "It is when your facts and persons grow unreal and fantastic by too much falsehood, that the scholar flies to the world of ideas, and aims to recruit and replenish nature from that source" (*CW* 1:146).

The scholar has a special obligation to give utterance to ideas, Emerson states in "The Method of Nature," another work of 1841, "in a country where the material interest is so predominant as it is in America." The fluctuation that Jacksonians decried in the currency he finds endemic to commercial society; he interprets it as an index of the lack of secure values in a culture preoccupied with speculation and the scramble for riches: "The rapid wealth which hundreds in the community acquire in trade, or by the incessant expansions of our population and arts, enchants the eyes of all the rest; the luck of one is the hope of thousands, and the proximity of the bribe acts like the neighborhood of a gold mine to impoverish the farm, the school, the church, the house, and the very body and feature of man" (*CW* 1 : 120). Although Emerson goes on to disclaim any animus against "the mart of commerce" (*CW* 1 : 120), it is evident that he regards the marketplace as the realm of instability and chance. Its revolutions impress him with the folly of putting faith in material possessions and contribute to his distrust of the physical world in general. "Self-Reliance," for example, makes the point that "reliance on Property . . . is the want of self-reliance" and mentions bankruptcies along with fire, storm, and mobs as occurrences over which men have little or no control (*CW* 2 : 49). The essay "Circles" (1841), which presents a sustained vision of a world in flux, adduces one of its earliest illustrations from the uncertainties of trade: "Every thing looks permanent until its secret is known. A rich estate appears to women a firm and lasting fact; to a merchant, one easily created out of any materials, and easily lost" (*CW* 2 : 180). Emerson's next illustration in this essay indicates that even land, now that it has been drawn into the exchange process, exhibits the instability of portable property; to the "large"—that is, market—farmer, it is as speculative an investment as a gold mine. "An orchard, good tillage, good grounds, seem a fixture, like a gold mine, or a river, to a citizen; to a large farmer, not much more fixed than the state of the crop" (*CW* 2 : 180).

"Circles" demonstrates in detail that the very possibility of "firm and lasting facts" is at issue in a cosmos where "there are no fixtures" and "all that we reckoned settled, shakes and rattles" (*CW* 2 : 179, 184). The world itself—or to speak more accurately, the phenomenal world—behaves as unpredictably as the marketplace. The death of Emerson's son in 1842 elicits a despairing acknowledgment that "the results of life are uncalculated and uncalculable" (*W* 3 : 69). In the essay "Experience" (1844), Emerson actually likens Waldo's death to the kind of economic setbacks that were so prevalent in antebellum America:

> Grief too will make us idealists. In the death of my son, now more than two years ago, I seem to have lost a beautiful estate—no more. I cannot get it nearer to me. If tomorrow I

should be informed of the bankruptcy of my principal debtors, the loss of my property would be a great inconvenience to me, perhaps, for many years; but it would leave me as it found me—neither better nor worse. So it is with this calamity. [*W* 3:48–49]

Although Emerson himself refuses to exalt fortune "into a divinity" (*W* 3:70), he recognizes that for most men the vicissitudes of life make it seem a game of chance, like commercial speculation. Hence his appeal at the conclusion of "Self-Reliance": "So use all that is called Fortune. Most men gamble with her, and gain all, and lose all, as her wheel rolls. But do thou leave as unlawful these winnings, and deal with Cause and Effect, the chancellors of God. In the Will work and acquire, and thou hast chained the wheel of Chance, and shall sit hereafter out of fear from her rotations" (*CW* 2:50).

Emerson's own tendencies toward Idealism were strengthened by the Crash of 1837. The collapse of the economy, which he records in his journal for April and May of that year, leads him to question the ultimate reality of matter. After noting details of bank failure and worsening unemployment, Emerson continues:

I see a good in such emphatic and universal calamity as the times bring, that they dissatisfy me with society. . . . Society has played out its last stake; it is check-mated. Young men have no hope. Adults stand like daylaborers idle in the streets. None calleth us to labor. . . . The present generation is bankrupt of principles and hope, as of property. . . . I am forced to ask if the Ideal might not also be tried. Is it to be taken for granted that it is impracticable? Behold the boasted world has come to nothing. . . . Behold . . . here is the Soul erect and Unconquered still.[11]

It is a short step from these remarks to the conclusion that nothing is reliable or permanent except the Soul. In fact Emerson had reached such a conclusion a year earlier in *Nature*, the first major statement of his Transcendentalism and a work, though it antedates the Panic, that provides the most complex and provocative exposition of his attitude toward the market.

It may seem curious to speak of *Nature* as a commentary on exchange society. The essay has been studied from virtually every perspective *but* this one, and although it was composed at a moment of intense ideological ferment, the climax of Jackson's struggle to destroy the Bank, it appears to take only indirect and passing notice of recent events. In a more general sense, however, the very first "use" of nature that Emerson considers, "Commodity," suggests his active interest in contemporary issues. A very different book, Marx's *Capital* (1867), similarly begins with an examination of "The Commodity"; and Emerson as well as Marx is concerned to make sense of, and ultimately to redeem, a world converted into articles of exchange. The structure of the essay reveals Emerson's strategy in this respect. As it proceeds from commodity to beauty, to language, to discipline, to idealism, and finally to spirit, the essay exhibits what has been called a "mounting dialectic," a movement from the concrete and physical to an affirmation of the spiritual basis of all reality.[12] In other words, Emerson will attempt to salvage the world as commodity by infusing it with the Soul.

To be sure, Emerson does not formulate his undertaking in *Nature* in exactly these terms. The task he assigns himself in the introductory section, to reconcile the visible universe and the Soul, is as old as philosophy itself. What is striking, however, is the view of nature which he sets forth under the heading of "Commodity." He suggests that nineteenth-century man has already approached reconciliation with the creation through technology and commerce. Writing of "those advantages which our senses owe to nature" (*CW* 1:11), Emerson pictures a thoroughly domesticated cosmos ministering incessantly to man, a cosmos where everything conspires to make him feel at home: "Beasts, fire, water, stones, and corn serve him. The field is at once his floor, his work-yard, his play-ground, his garden, and his bed." Two lines from George Herbert's "Man" add poetic emphasis—

> More servants wait on man
> Than he'll take notice of.

—and a paragraph-long account of the "useful arts" celebrates technology's role in promoting progress:

> He [man] no longer waits for favoring gales, but by means of steam, he realizes the fable of Aeolus's bag, and carries the two and thirty winds in the boiler of his boat. To diminish friction, he paves the road with iron bars, and, mounting a coach with a ship-load of men, animals, and merchandise behind him, he darts through the country, from town to town, like an eagle or a swallow through the air. By the aggregate of these aids, how

is the face of the world changed, from the era of Noah to that of Napoleon! The private poor man hath cities, shops, canals, bridges, built for him. He goes to the post-office, and the human race run on his errands; to the book-shop, and the human race read and write of all that happens, for him; to the court-house, and nations repair his wrongs. He sets his house upon the road, and the human race go forth every morning, and shovel out the snow, and cut a path for him. [*CW* 1 : 11–12]

It would be hard to imagine a more enthusiastic assessment of the developments that Emerson would deplore, two years later, as the "invasion of Nature by Trade with its Money, its Steam, its Railroad." The market aided by technology puts all things into motion and creates a world that is portable as well as tractable to human purposes. The very ground under man's feet has become fluid like the sea or the air: hence the reference to transporting "shiploads" of produce by rail and traversing the country with the speed of "an eagle or a swallow." The "changed face" that the modern world wears is very much a human countenance; looking about him, man beholds a universe that seems his own product and mirrors back his image. When, in the "Discipline" section, Emerson returns briefly to the benefits of the commodity, he sums up nature's relation to man as one of duplication. Nature, he says, "offers all its kingdoms to man as the raw material which he may mould into what is useful. Man is never weary of working it up . . . until the world becomes, at last, only a realized will—the double of man" (*CW* 1 : 25).

Nature may be thought of as possessing three distinct stages, and in this, the first stage, the humanization of the "Not-Me" lies well within man's power. A radically opposed view of man's relation to his cosmos emerges from the essay's second stage. Emerson has insisted from the beginning that nature's material benefits are "mercenary" (*CW* 1 : 12), that "the use of Commodity, regarded by itself, is mean and squalid" (*CW* 1 : 26). This negative note, which grows more emphatic as the argument progresses, culminates in a vision of the physical world as alien and debased. It leads Emerson, in the section on "Idealism," to entertain his "noble doubt": "whether nature outwardly exists." And although he determines to leave open the question of matter's absolute existence, he resolves "to regard nature as a phenomenon, not a substance; to attribute necessary existence to spirit; to esteem nature as an accident and an effect" (*CW* 1 : 29–30).

Emerson's revulsion from commodity is so great that he even identifies the visible creation with scum or dross, and implicitly with excrement. In the "Language" section, he describes facts as "the end or last issue of spirit" and quotes approvingly from a French Swedenborgian, G. Oegger, whose *True Messiah* he had read in a manuscript translation: "'Material objects are necessarily kinds of *scoriae* of the substantial thoughts of the Creator, which must always preserve an exact relation to their first origin; in other words, visible nature must have a spiritual and moral side'" (*CW* 1:22–23). *Scoriae* are the slag thrown off from metals in the process of smelting; the word derives from the Greek for feces and has scatological overtones of which Emerson, as a classical scholar, would surely have been aware. That he makes this association may help to explain why he is so ready, in the "Introduction," to construe his own body as the Not-Me. Equally important, the quotation from Oegger points up the link between seeing the world as commodity, and thus potentially as "filthy lucre," and holding it in contempt. It has been argued, for example, that there exists a close connection between the rise of capitalism in the sixteenth century and Lutheran Protestantism's rejection of the world as excrement, as utterly corrupt and worthless.[13] Three centuries later, Emerson similarly devalues matter and equates it with *scoriae* precisely because the market has transformed it into objects exchangeable for money.

Man's relation to an excremental universe turns out to be one not of mastery but of estrangement. Far from feeling at home in the world, most men, according to Emerson, "abdicate [their] kingdom" and "creep into a corner" (*CW* 1:15). And despite his earlier paean to technology, Emerson claims that nature is "not . . . now subjected to the human will" (*CW* 1:38). The fault lies more in man than in the creation. Because men commonly relate to nature as commodity, they fail to apprehend its "spiritual and moral side" and only deepen their alienation even as they subdue the physical world: "The ruin or blank, that we see when we look at nature, is in our own eye" (*CW* 1:43). "As we degenerate, the contrast between us and our house is more evident. We are as much strangers in nature, as we are aliens from God" (*CW* 1:39). In the same vein Emerson's Orphic poet characterizes man's present condition as "a god in ruins." Once, the poet sings,

> [man] filled nature with his overflowing currents. . . . But, having made for himself this huge shell, his waters retired; he no longer fills the veins and veinlets; he is shrunk to a drop. He

sees, that the structure still fits him, but fits him colossally. Say, rather, once it fitted him, now it corresponds to him from far and on high. He adores timidly his own work. . . . Yet sometimes he starts in his slumber, and wonders at himself and his house, and muses strangely at the resemblance betwixt him and it. [*CW* 1 : 42]

These sentiments form a complete contrast to the affirmations of "Commodity." Harmony between man and his world, the ostensible goal of economic and technological progress, is said to lie in the past rather than the future. "And all history," declares the poet, "is but the epoch of one degradation" (*CW* 1 : 42).

In the third stage of *Nature* Emerson reclaims the world for nineteenth-century man. He argues that Reason or intuition enables men to apprehend the spiritual element that pervades the universe and heals the breach between mind and matter. Because all objects in the world have a spiritual as well as a material side, nature is not alien but emblematic and charged with meaning to the eye of Reason: "Every natural fact is a symbol of some spiritual fact. Every appearance in nature corresponds to some state of the mind, and that state of the mind can only be described by presenting that natural appearance as its picture" (*CW* 1 : 18). The poet in particular, with his highly developed imagination, has the gift of discerning "this radical correspondence between visible things and human thoughts" (*CW* 1 : 19). Using nature symbolically for purposes of expression, he "unfixes the land and the sea . . . and disposes them anew." "The sensual man conforms thoughts to things; the poet conforms things to his thoughts. The one esteems nature as rooted and fast; the other, as fluid, and impresses his being thereon" (*CW* 1 : 31).

What the poet does figuratively, moreover, all men can do in actuality by grasping "that wonderful congruity which subsists" between them and the cosmos (*CW* 1 : 40). They can overcome their alienation and make nature serve their wishes by exercising the spiritual authority to which it is obedient. In Emerson's words, "behind nature, throughout nature, spirit is present . . . it does not act upon us from without . . . but spiritually, or through ourselves. Therefore . . . spirit, that is, the Supreme Being, does not build up nature around us, but puts it forth through us. . . . [We are] nourished by unfailing fountains" and have at our command "inexhaustible power." "Who can set bounds to the possibilities of man?" (*CW* 1 : 38), Emerson exclaims rhetorically, and he envisions through his Orphic poet the imminent realization of "the kingdom of man over nature . . . a dominion such as now is beyond his dream of God" (*CW* 1:45).

For Emerson, in sum, the taint of commodity is transcended by spiritualizing matter and exchanging it for meaning instead of money. As this procedure suggests, he remains unwittingly indebted to the marketplace. In economic terms, a commodity has both use value and exchange value; similarly in Emerson's terms, things both exist in their own right and stand for something else.[14] Indeed, the whole third step of Emerson's argument in *Nature* reveals his profound ambivalence about the market economy. It makes clear just how much there is in common between treating nature as commodity and "degrading nature"—a favorite word of Emerson's in this connection— by "suggesting its dependence on spirit" (*CW* 1:35).

Although Emerson rejects commerce as a way to unify the Me and Not-Me, he betrays his admiration for it in his conception of the Soul. For spirit functions exactly like the market to domesticate the world and make it portable: to transform the creation into "the double of man." In "Commodity" nature is at once man's floor, his workyard, his playground, his garden, and his bed; in the "Prospects" section, which prophesies reunification through spirit, the world is his house:

Nature is not fixed but fluid. Spirit alters, moulds, makes it. The immobility or bruteness of nature is the absence of spirit; to pure spirit, it is volatile, it is obedient. Every spirit builds itself a house; and beyond its house, a world; and beyond its world, a heaven. Know then, that the world exists for you. For you is the phenomenon perfect. What we are, that only can we see. All that Adam had, all that Caesar could, you have and can do. Adam called his house, heaven and earth; Caesar called his house, Rome; you perhaps call yours, a cobler's trade; a hundred acres of ploughed land; or a scholar's garret. Yet, line for line and point for point, your dominion is as great as theirs, though without fine names. Build, therefore, your own world. [*CW* 1:44–45]

The malleability of nature, of which the Orphic poet sings here, is a commonplace of Romantic thought. In the context established by Emerson, however, the poet's song is a mimicry of the capitalist spirit it otherwise condemns. The references to Adam and Caesar further illuminate the dual impulses that inform the essay. The references suggest two altogether different approaches to nature, peaceful coexistence and ruthless domination, and they point simultaneously to the agrarian past and the capitalist future. In other writings Emerson himself compares the farmer to Adam, and the figure who reminds him most of Caesar, Napoleon Bonaparte, appears in *Representative Men* (1850) as the champion of the commercial middle class.[15]

Nature bears out Emerson's own assertion, made in a lecture on literature in 1837, that "the great political and economical revolution which has transpired . . . is very conspicuously traced in letters."[16] The agrarianism he shares with the Jacksonians tells only half the story of his relation to them and to the age. As Meyers emphasizes, it tells only half the story of the Jacksonians' own feelings about the economic revolution they both advanced and denounced. Characterizing them as "venturous conservatives," Meyers writes that "the Jacksonians wanted to preserve the virtues of a simple agrarian republic without sacrificing the rewards and conveniences of modern capitalism."[17] Something very similar might be said of *Nature*. Disavowing, on the one hand, the commercial outlook of the times, Emerson, on the other, purifies and sanctions an aggressive, "capitalistic" ethos of mastery over nature.[18]

The essay "Compensation," published in 1841 but conceived as early as 1826, provides an even more extreme illustration of this tension in Emerson's thought. It begins with several paragraphs in which he heaps scorn upon "the base estimate of the market." He describes having heard a minister preach a sermon on the Last Judgment which pictured the wicked as thriving in this life and promised the saints eventual compensation for their sufferings "by giving them," in Emerson's sarcastic gloss, "the like gratifications another day—bank-stock and doubloons, venison and champagne." The minister's error, he adds, "lay in the immense concession that the bad are successful; that justice is not done now" (*CW* 2:56). But having dismissed as shortsighted an economic standard of success—"every crime is punished," he contends, "every virtue rewarded . . . in silence and certainty" (*CW* 2:60)—Emerson replaces it with an ethical theory that seems almost to parody the accounting procedures of the marketplace.

Emerson's very language, including the title of his essay, bespeaks a predilection to find economic categories applicable to the operations of the Soul. With undisguised admiration for the proverbs "hourly preached in all markets and workshops," he insists, "the doctrine that every thing has its price . . . is not less sublime in the columns of a leger than . . . in all the action and reaction of nature" (*CW* 2:64,

67). Because "a third silent party" participates in "all our bargains," and the "soul of things takes on itself the guaranty of the fulfillment of every contract," no vicious action can result in gain, no honest conduct "come to loss" (*CW* 2:69). God himself, in his view, is a kind of supremely efficient bookkeeper who "makes square the eternal account" (*CW* 2:70): "The longer the payment is withholden, the better for you; for compound interest on compound interest is the rate and usage of this exchequer" (*CW* 2:69). Here, and with a vengeance, is the commercialization of all things, the very attitude Emerson objected to in the preacher's sermon on the Judgment Day. Once again, the best commentary on this frame of mind, which seems unable to distinguish between natural law and the market regime ("in Nature, nothing can be given, all things are sold" [*CW* 2:63]), comes from Emerson himself and appears in the essay "Worship" from *The Conduct of Life* (1860): "Heaven always bears some proportion to earth. The god of the cannibals will be a cannibal, of the crusaders a crusader, and of the merchants a merchant" (*W* 6:205).

"Compensation" reveals an Emerson already well on his way to becoming an apologist for commercial and industrial capitalism. His criticisms of trade as degrading and capricious decline in importance until they largely disappear by the Civil War. His defense of the market as rational and even spiritual in its operations, the view implicit in *Nature* and "Compensation," grows more dominant in the same period, even as laissez-faire ideology proves increasingly influential in American culture. This favorable view is especially strong in a work like "Wealth," where Emerson repudiates the radical "excesses" of his early thought and glorifies worldly success as a sign of spiritual election. The implications of *Nature* attain a curious and perhaps inevitable fulfillment in this essay, as Emerson attributes to great wealth the very powers that he once ascribed to spirit. Money rather than the Soul wins praise for its ability to confer "command over nature" (*W* 6:96) and to enable its possessor to implement his vision: "Men of sense esteem wealth to be the assimilation of nature to themselves, the converting of the sap and juices of the planet to the incarnation and nutriment of their design. Power is what they want . . . power to execute their design, power to give legs and feet, form and actuality to their thought" (*W* 6:93).

Since "wealth is moral" (*W* 6:103), moreover, riches advertise their owner as a man of character. Under the market system, whose workings are as dependable as the laws of nature, "property rushes from the idle and imbecile to the industrious, brave and persevering"

(*W* 6:106). Commerce is still a game, according to Emerson, but "a game of skill" in which chance plays no part: "There is always a reason, *in the man*, for his good or bad fortune, and so in making money. Men talk as if there were some magic about this . . . [But the successful entrepreneur] knows that all goes on the old road, pound for pound, cent for cent—for every effect a perfect cause—and that good luck is another name for tenacity of purpose" (*W* 6:100). Self-reliance, once seen as threatened by "commercial times," is now said to flourish in the unregulated marketplace; the enterprising individual who has done his work faithfully "can well afford not to conciliate" and "contracts no stain" from the exchange process (*W* 6:92). In "Wealth" Emerson gives highest marks to the independence enjoyed by the rich man, not the husbandman, and he depicts as obsolete the ideal of self-sufficiency associated in "Man the Reformer" with the farm: "When men now alive were born, the farm yielded everything that was consumed on it. The farm yielded no money, and the farmer got on without. If he fell sick, his neighbors came in to his aid; each gave a day's work, or a half day . . . hoed his potatoes, mowed his hay, reaped his rye; well knowing that no man could afford to hire labor without selling his land. . . . Now, the farmer buys almost all he consumes—tinware, cloth, sugar, tea, coffee, fish, coal, railroad tickets and newspapers" (*W* 6:118–19).

The Jeffersonian tradition is no longer alive in the Emerson of *The Conduct of Life*. Even a work like "Farming," written around the same time and often anthologized as an example of Emerson's agrarianism,[19] in fact only shows how far he has traveled from this strain in his original philosophy. Although the essay pays tribute to the farmer for his industry and closeness to nature, it also compares him, in a truly astonishing image, to the boy who watches the loom in an English factory and is known as "a minder." It pictures nature, not as fluid and volatile, but as a "machine . . . of colossal proportions . . . [that] is never out of gear" (*W* 7:142). The farmer can hardly be considered a model of independence if he is a figurative factory hand, and it is clear that husbandry has ceased to have this significance for Emerson. He now thinks of farming as a refuge from the cares of city life:

> All men keep the farm in reserve as an asylum where, in case of mischance, to hide their poverty—or a solitude, if they do not succeed in society. And who knows how many glances of remorse are turned this way from the bankrupts of trade, from

mortified pleaders in courts and senates, or from the victims of idleness and pleasure? Poisoned by town life and town vices, the sufferer resolves: "Well, my children, whom I have injured, shall go back to the land, and be recruited and cured by that which should have been my nursery, and now shall be their hospital." [*W* 7:132]

What deserves emphasis in this passage is the evaporation of the agrarian ethos as a viable social or economic faith. Twenty years earlier Emerson used husbandry as a metaphor for a kind of personal autonomy that seemed jeopardized by the growth of the market; he uses it here as a metaphor for withdrawal and recuperation from capitalist civilization. An escape rather than a critical vantage point, it has become irrelevant to a society based on money.

If the vitality of the agrarian ideal, with its antimarket bias, does not survive in Emerson himself, however, it is carried on by his "disciple" Thoreau. And Emerson, with the irritation of a mentor whose most promising follower reproaches him for apostasy, is at pains to reply to Thoreau's experiment in *Walden*. In "Man the Reformer" he called upon his listeners to "learn the meaning of economy" and commended "parched corn and a house with one apartment" as a discipline in freedom (*CW* 1:154). Thoreau seems to have mastered the lesson altogether too well for Emerson's equanimity in "Wealth." Beginning with the question, "How does that man get his living?" (*W* 6:85)—precisely the question Thoreau sought to answer in writing *Walden*—Emerson disparages a life of "bare subsistence" and takes issue with his erstwhile pupil's doctrine of simplicity: "It is of no use to argue the wants down: the philosophers have laid the greatness of man in making his wants few, but will a man content himself with a hut and a handful of dried pease? He is born to be rich" (*W* 6:88). In *Walden* Thoreau says, "Enjoy the land, but own it not," aware that in a commercial society the very fact of ownership involves one in the process of exchange.[20] Emerson evidently has him in mind when he declares in "Wealth," "No land is bad, but land is worse," and goes on to explain that farming and scholarship are incompatible: "this pottering in a few square yards of garden is dispiriting and drivelling. . . . [The scholar] grows peevish and poor-spirited. The genius of reading and of gardening are antagonistic, like resinous and vitreous electricity. One is concentrative in sparks and shocks; the other is diffuse strength; so that each disqualifies its workman for the other's duties" (*W* 6:116). Although Emerson is speaking here of reading, his strictures presumably apply to writing as well. As such, they amount to a rejection of Thoreau's most urgent project in *Walden*, his attempt to overcome the division of labor in his own person by uniting husbandry and literature and to formulate a conception of the writer that will exempt him from the "curse of trade." To which Emerson rejoins, in a phrase already partly quoted, that great art—the most individual of all commodities—"contracts no stain from the market, but makes the market a silent gallery for itself" (*W* 6:92).

2

Walden and the "Curse of Trade"

I

A mong the many paradoxes of *Walden* perhaps none is more ironic than the fact that this modernist text—modernist in its celebration of private consciousness, its aestheticizing of experience, its demands upon the reader—starts out as a denunciation of modernity. It is inspired by the agrarian ideals of the past, yet in making a metaphor of those ideals it fails as a rejoinder to the nineteenth century and creates as many problems as it lays to rest. Personal and historical disappointment determines the shape of Thoreau's masterpiece. In important ways it is a defeated text. Though Thoreau begins with the conviction that literature can change the world, the aesthetic strategies he adopts to accomplish political objectives involve him in a series of withdrawals from history; in each case the ahistorical maneuver disables the political and is compromised by the very historical moment it seeks to repudiate.

This is not to deny *Walden*'s greatness, but rather to emphasize the cost of Thoreau's achievement and to begin to specify its limits. No reader of the book can fail to notice the exultant tone of the "Conclusion"; the impression it leaves is of an author who has made good on his promise not to write "an ode to dejection" (p. 84).[1] But one might say, in another paradox, that *Walden*'s triumphant success is

This chapter is to appear in a slightly revised form in *Ideology and American Literature: The Mid-nineteenth Century*, ed. Sacvan Bercovitch and Myra Jehlen (New York: Cambridge University Press, forthcoming).

precisely what constitutes its defeat. For underlying that triumph is a forsaking of civic aspirations for an exclusive concern with "the art of living well" (in Emerson's phrase about his former disciple).[2] And to say this is to suggest that *Walden* is a book at odds with its own beliefs; it is to point out Thoreau's complicity in the ideological universe he abhors.

II

At the heart of Thoreau's dissent from modernity is a profound hostility to the process of exchange, to what he calls the "curse of trade" (p. 70). He pictures a contemporary Concord where everyone is implicated in the market, and he mounts a critique of that society as antithetical to independence, to identity, and to life itself. His antimarket attitude, though it has similarities to pastoralism,[3] is more properly understood as a nineteenth-century revision of the agrarian or civic humanist tradition. Civic humanists regarded the economic autonomy of the individual as the basis for his membership in the polis. The self-sufficient owner of the soil, in their view, was the ideal citizen because he relied on his own property and exertions for his livelihood and was virtually immune to compromising pressures. Commercial enterprise, in contrast, endangered liberty because it fostered dependence on others and, by legitimating the pursuit of private interest, undermined devotion to the common good. Jeffersonian agrarianism, the American development of this tradition, retained its antimarket bias and its stress on freedom from the wills of others. In Jefferson's own formulation from the *Notes on the State of Virginia*, commerce is productive of subservience, and the independent husbandman uniquely capable of civic virtue.[4]

Thoreau, writing some sixty years after Jefferson, shows a similar antipathy to exchange but entertains no illusions about either the present-day husbandman or the benefits conferred by real property. Several pages into *Walden* appears his well-known indictment of the various forms of ingratiation and venality practiced by his neighbors in order to make money—an indictment that applies to the farmer as much as to the tradesman.

> It is very evident what mean and sneaking lives many of
> you live, . . . always promising to pay, promising to pay, to-
> morrow, and dying to-day, insolvent; seeking to curry favor to
> get custom, by how many modes, only not state-prison of-

fences; lying, flattering, voting [cf. Thoreau's attack on democracy in "Civil Disobedience"], contracting yourselves into a nutshell of civility, or dilating into an atmosphere of thin and vaporous generosity, that you may persuade your neighbor to let you make his shoes, or his hat, or his coat, or import his groceries for him. [Pp. 6–7]

Thoreau's position in this passage is directly opposed to the laissez-faire ideology gaining in popularity among his contemporaries. He sees the marketplace (not) as a discipline in self-reliance, an arena where the man of enterprise can prove his worth, but rather as a site of humiliation where the seller has to court and conciliate potential buyers to gain their custom. The interactions of exchange, in his view, breed not independence but servility. Nor, insists Thoreau, does nineteenth-century agriculture offer an exemption from the abasements and dependencies of the exchange process. The land has become an investment like any other and the farmer a willing participant in the marketplace. The husbandmen of Concord, immortalized by Emerson for their stand "by the rude bridge that arched the flood," are now "serfs of the soil" who spend their lives "buying and selling" and have forgotten the meaning of self-reliance (pp. 5, 208). Thoreau envisions them, in a celebrated image, "creeping down the road of life," each pushing before him "a barn seventy-five feet by forty . . . and one hundred acres of land, tillage, mowing, pasture, and wood-lot!" (p. 5).

For Thoreau, commercial agriculture has an impact on the physical world which is just as devastating as its effect on the farmer. In the chapter "The Ponds" he describes an agricultural entrepreneur named Flint for whom nature exists solely as commodity. Indeed, on Flint's farm the use value of natural objects has been consumed by their exchange value; their abstract character as potential money has completely obliterated their "sensuous" reality (to use a favorite adjective of Marx's in this connection) as fruits and vegetables. The result is an impoverishment of the thing, an alteration of its very nature. "I respect not his labors," Thoreau writes of Flint,

> his farm where every thing has its price; who would carry the landscape, who would carry his God, to market, if he could get any thing for him; . . . on whose farm nothing grows free, whose fields bear no crops, whose meadows no flowers, whose trees no fruits, but dollars; who loves not the beauty of his

fruits, whose fruits are not ripe for him till they are turned to
dollars. [P. 196]

A companion chapter, "The Pond in Winter," shows this destruc-
tion of nature actually coming to pass through the speculations of "a
gentleman farmer" who carries the landscape off to market. Wanting
"to cover each one of his dollars with another," the farmer has hired a
crew of laborers to strip Walden of its ice. Thoreau treats the entire
operation as though the ice-cutters were "busy husbandmen" engaged in skimming the land: "They went to work at once, plough-
ing, harrowing, rolling, furrowing . . . [and] suddenly began to hook
up the virgin mould itself, with a peculiar jerk, clear down to the
sand, or rather the water, . . . all the *terra firma* there was, and haul it
away on sleds" (pp. 294–95).

As Thoreau's denunciation of Flint makes clear, his quarrel with
the marketplace is in large measure ontological. He sees the exchange
process as emptying the world of its concrete reality and not only
converting objects into dollars but causing their "it-ness" or being to
disappear. A particularly powerful statement of this idea occurs at the
beginning of "The Ponds," in the passage (cited in Chapter 1) where
Thoreau assails the marketing of huckleberries. He argues that nature's fruits "do not yield their true flavor" either to the man who
raises them commercially or to their urban purchasers. The huckleberry cannot be tasted or even said to exist outside its native habitat:
invariably it undergoes a fatal transformation en route from the
countryside to the metropolis. What reaches Boston is not the fra-
grant berry itself but the "mere provender" that the fruit has become
in being transported to the customer. Its bloom has been "rubbed off
in the market cart" and its "ambrosial and essential part" extinguished
by its conversion into an article of trade (p. 173).

Thoreau believes that along with the degradation of the physical
object in exchange there occurs a shriveling of the individual. Men in
the marketplace, according to *Walden*, do not relate as persons but as
something less than human; they commit violence against their own
natures in their incessant anxiety to induce others to buy their products or their labor. "The finest qualities of our nature," Thoreau says
in a passage paralleling his discussion of the huckleberry, "like the
bloom on fruits, can be preserved only by the most delicate handling.
Yet we do not treat ourselves or one another thus tenderly" (p. 6).
The laborer's self, his authentic being, has as little chance to survive
the exchange process as a genuine huckleberry. To satisfy his em-

ployer, he has to suppress his individuality and become a mechanical thing: "Actually, the laboring man has not leisure for a true integrity day by day; he cannot afford to sustain the manliest relations to men; his labor would be depreciated in the market. He has no time to be anything but a machine" (p. 6). The final disappearance of the person, the most extreme form of absence, would be death, and Thoreau does in fact equate exchange with the deprivation of life. "The cost of a thing," he writes, "is the amount of what I will call life which is required to be exchanged for it, immediately or in the long run" (p. 31). Exchange brings about the ultimate alienation of man from himself; to engage in buying and selling is not merely to debase the self but to extinguish it, to hurry into death.

Thoreau's analysis of commodification has certain affinities with the Marxist critique of capitalism. His comments on the erosion of human presence in exchange evoke the notion of reification, a concept developed in the twentieth century by Georg Lukács. Reification refers to the phenomenon whereby a social relation between men assumes the character of a relation between things. Because they interact through the commodities they exchange, including the commodity of labor, individuals in the capitalist market confront each other not as human beings, but as objectified, nonhuman entities. They lose sight altogether of the subjective element in their activity. An important corollary to this loss of the person is a confusion of history with nature. By mystifying or obscuring man's involvement in the production of his social reality, reification leads him to apprehend that reality as a "second nature." He perceives the social realm as an immutable and universal order over which he exerts no control. The result is greatly to diminish the possibility of human freedom.[5]

Thoreau reaches a similar conclusion about the decline of liberty under capitalism: he portrays his townsmen as slave-drivers of themselves. The weakness of his position, a weakness to which we shall return, is that he launches his attack against history rather than in its name, with the result that he mystifies the temporality of his own experience, presenting it as natural or removed from social time. He is outspoken in debunking such "naturalization" when it functions as a way of legitimating social codes. In his disquisition on clothing, for example, he points out how the fetishism of fashion invests the merely whimsical with the prestige of inevitability. "When I ask for a garment of a particular form," he explains, "my tailoress tells me gravely, 'They do not make them so now,' not emphasizing the 'They' at all, as if she quoted an authority as impersonal as the Fates. . . . We worship not the Graces, nor the Parcae, but Fashion" (p. 25).

Thoreau constantly challenges the false identification of what "they" say or do with the course of nature. He maintains that social reality, to which men submit as though to "a seeming fate" (p. 5), is in fact made by men and subject to their revision. His neighbors, whose resignation only masks their desperation, do not adopt the customary modes of living out of preference but "honestly think there is no choice left" (p. 8). Although they deny the possibility of change and say, "This is the only way," Thoreau insists that they are mistaken, that "there are as many ways" to live as "can be drawn radii from one centre" (p. 11). His lack of deference toward his elders stems from the same impatience with a reified social reality. Old people, he finds, regard their own experience as exemplary and refuse even to contemplate alternatives to the existing order of things. But "what old people say you cannot do you try and find that you can" (p. 8). What they fail to realize, what Thoreau feels all his neighbors are unable to see, is that "their daily life of routine and habit . . . is built on purely illusory foundations." They "think that *is* which *appears* to be" (p. 96).

III

To negate the "curse of trade" during his stay in the woods, Thoreau supports himself by farming. This is the occupation followed by the majority of his neighbors, but his own experiment in husbandry differs significantly from the commercial agriculture prevalent in Concord. By building his own house and growing his own food, by concentrating on the necessaries of life and renouncing luxuries, he minimizes his dependency on others and removes himself as far as possible from the market economy. In keeping with his precept, "Enjoy the land, but own it not" (p. 207), he squats on soil belonging to someone else (Emerson, as it happens) and endeavors to "avoid all trade and barter" (p. 64). "More independent than any farmer in Concord," he claims to have learned from his experience that something approaching self-sufficiency is still practicable in mid-nineteenth-century America, if only "one would live simply and eat only the crop which he raised, and raise no more than he ate, and not exchange it for an insufficient quantity of more luxurious and expensive things" (pp. 55–56).

Something *approaching* self-sufficiency: Thoreau makes no attempt to disguise the fact that he is unable to emancipate himself completely from exchange relations. He freely "publishes his guilt," as he puts it (p. 59), that his venture at subsistence farming is not strictly speaking an economic success. He raises a cash crop of beans and uses the proceeds to give variety to his diet, and he is forced to supplement his income from farming by hiring himself out as a day laborer, the employment he finds "the most independent of any, especially as it required only thirty to forty days in a year to support one" (p. 70). He recognizes, in other words, the obsolescence of his program as a *literal* antidote to the ills of market civilization.

What Thoreau does affirm, and affirm consistently, is the possibility even in the nineteenth century of a way of life characterized by self-reliance and minimal involvement in exchange. Following the civic humanist tradition, he identifies this ideal with husbandry, and husbandry in turn supplies him with a metaphoric solution to the problems of the marketplace. Agriculture, he states, "was once a sacred art; but it is pursued with irreverent haste and heedlessness by us, our object being to have large farms and large crops merely" (p. 165). Thoreau makes a point of actually farming in the traditional way,[6] going down to the woods and living by himself, because he refuses to sacrifice the use value of husbandry to its symbolic value in the manner of Flint. He wants to earn his metaphor by dwelling "near enough to Nature and Truth to borrow a trope from them" (p. 245).

Thoreau has an acute sense of the relationship between commodity and symbolism—or rather of the commodified thinking concealed in symbolization. The commodity, like the symbol, is both what it is and the token of something else (i.e., money); on Flint's farm, the something else has totally displaced the concrete reality. To use farming as a trope for self-sufficiency without literally farming would be to perform in thought the same violation Flint commits on his land. Thoreau finds this commodified habit of mind to be the common practice of his contemporaries. "Our lives," he complains, "pass at such remoteness from its symbols, and its metaphors and tropes are so far fetched" (pp. 244–45). At Walden he redeems his own life from such distancing and loss of the real; he farms the land, as he says in "The Bean-Field," "for the sake of tropes and expression, to serve a parable-maker one day" (p. 162).[7]

Thoreau suggests that the values formerly associated with farming are available to all men, in all pursuits. "Labor of the hands," as he describes his hoeing, ". . . has a constant and imperishable moral, and to the scholar it yields a classic result" (p. 157). The moral yielded by *Walden* is that virtually any kind of workman can be a figurative farmer and any kind of work independent "labor of the hands." The centrality of this phrase to Thoreau's undertaking is suggested by its position at the very outset of the book; it appears in the opening sentence: "When I wrote the following pages, or rather the bulk of them, I lived alone, in the woods, a mile from any neighbor, in a house which I had built myself, on the shore of Walden Pond, in Concord, Massachusetts, and earned my living by the labor of my hands only" (p. 3). Labor of the hands is clearly meant to encompass intellectual as well as manual work. As Thoreau says in explaining what he lived for, "My head is hands and feet. I feel all my best faculties concentrated in it" (p. 98).

A difficulty that arises immediately with Thoreau's metaphoric solution to exchange is that it has the effect of privatizing a civic virtue. Farming as a way of life enjoyed the high standing it did in civic humanist thought because it was a training for participation in the public or political sphere. In *Walden*, as a figure for self-reliant labor, it has become a private virtue—a virtue without civic consequences. And there is no doubt that Thoreau hoped his text would result in some form of political awakening. Indeed, one of his principal objectives in writing *Walden* is to restore his countrymen to the freedom which they have lost under the market system. He moves to the woods on "Independence Day, or the fourth of July, 1845" because he considers this a civic enterprise, requiring a reformation or new foundation of American liberty (p. 84). A close connection can be seen here between the project of *Walden* and Thoreau's appeal at the end of "Civil Disobedience" for a founder or reformer whose eloquence will revive the polity. In the essay, which he wrote while working on the early drafts of the book, he criticizes the country's lawmakers for their failure to "speak with authority" about the government. Implicitly he projects a role for himself as a model legislator, one whose effectiveness will lie in his ability to inspire others through his words:

No man with a genius for legislation has appeared in America. They are rare in the history of the world. There are orators, politicians, and eloquent men, by the thousand; but the speaker has not yet opened his mouth to speak, who is capable

of settling the much-vexed questions of the day. We love eloquence for its own sake, and not for any truth which it may
utter, or any heroism it may inspire.[8]

In *Walden* Thoreau assumes the duties of this reformer-legislator
as a writer rather than a speaker because of the greater range and authority of literature. The orator, he says in the chapter "Reading,"
addresses the mob on the transitory issues of the moment, but the
author "speaks to the heart and intellect of mankind, to all in any age
who can *understand* him" (p. 102). Great writers, he adds, "are a natural and irresistible aristocracy in every society, and, more than kings
or emperors, exert an influence on mankind" (p. 103). Twentieth-
century readers, with their very different ideas about the functions of
texts and the role of the writer, may find it difficult to take these statements seriously. But it is a mistake to treat *Walden* as though it were
imbued with the modernist sentiment (to paraphrase W. H. Auden)
that literature makes nothing happen. This kind of accommodation
with "reality"—of reified consciousness—is precisely what Thoreau
is arguing against in the book. Nor for the time and place is there
anything especially unusual about his civic ambitions; on the contrary, they are perfectly consistent with the New England ideal of the
literary vocation.

Lewis P. Simpson has shown that a conception of the writer as a
spiritual and intellectual authority was particularly strong around
Boston and Concord during the early decades of the nineteenth century. Simpson uses the term "clerisy," a borrowing from Coleridge,
to designate the literary community that emerged at this time and
sought to claim for men of letters the influence formerly exercised by
the ministry. The wise and learned, it was felt, had a special obligation to educate the nation; through the practice of literature, they
were to provide moral guidance and enlightenment.[9] While Thoreau
was hardly a conventional member of the New England elite, he
shared his culture's emphasis on the usefulness of the literary calling.
He conceives *Walden* as a reforming text meant to produce results in
the world, and hopes to be remembered, like the heroic writers whom
he so admires, as a "messenger from heaven, [a] bearer of divine gifts
to man" (p. 36).

But in this respect *Walden* is a notably different text from "Civil
Disobedience": though both works begin, as it were, in the social
world, *Walden* retreats into the self while "Civil Disobedience" calls
for resistance to the government. This change can be seen in the

book's very structure, its transition from "Economy" to "Conclusion," from Concord and Thoreau's neighbors to the inwardness of self-discovery. A mood of withdrawal totally dominates the final pages, as Thoreau urges his readers to turn their backs on society and look inside themselves. "Be a Columbus to whole new continents and worlds within you," he exhorts, "opening new channels, not of trade, but of thought. . . . [E]xplore the private sea, the Atlantic and Pacific Ocean of [your] being alone" (p. 321). The ending contains some of the book's best-known aphorisms, most of which revolve around the sentiment that "every one [should] mind his own business, and endeavor to be what he was made" (p. 326). The image left is of a solitary individual pursuing his own development, cultivating his own consciousness, in utter indifference to the common good. Such an image is not only radically at odds with the tone of *Walden*'s beginning; it also amounts to a distorted—and reified—reflection of the laissez-faire individualist pursuing his private economic interest at the expense of the public welfare.

Thoreau's unwitting kinship with social behavior he deplores can also be seen in his effort to create a myth of his experience. As the narrative progresses, he seems to grow intent upon suppressing all traces of autobiography and treating his two years at the pond as a timeless and universal experience. The patterning of the book after the cycle of the seasons contributes to this sense of the mythological, as does perhaps even more strongly the almost purely metaphorical character of the "Conclusion." In contrast to the specificity of the opening chapter, which takes place in Concord, Massachusetts, in the year 1845, the ending is situated in no time and no physical location. Thoreau declares open war on history: after ridiculing the "transient and fleeting" doings of his contemporaries, he vows "not to live in this restless, nervous, bustling, trivial Nineteenth Century, but stand or sit thoughtfully while it goes by" (pp. 329–30). The text's denial of history, its flight from Jacksonian America, paradoxically resembles the commodified mode of thought which Thoreau charges against his countrymen and which permits a Flint to perceive his fruits and vegetables as dollars. In an analogous way, Thoreau allows the mythic value of his Walden experiment to displace the actual circumstances of its occurrence. Moreover, his determination to empty his adventure of historical content replicates a basic feature of reified consciousness. As he himself has pointed out repeatedly, market society engenders a conflation of history with nature. By presenting its limited, time-bound conventions as eternal, the existing order in effect places itself outside time and beyond the possibility of change. Although Thoreau rigorously condemns his society's "naturalizing" of itself in this fashion, he can be charged with performing a version of the same process on his own life by erasing history from *Walden* and mythologizing his experiment at the pond.[10]

IV

The privatizing and antihistorical tendencies which blunt *Walden*'s critical edge reappear in Thoreau's attempt to devise a conception of reading and writing as unalienated labor. He is obliged to seek such a formulation because as a maker of texts, a would-be reformer in literature, he encounters the same problem that his neighbors experience in their daily transactions as farmers, merchants, and workmen: he has to confront the specter of the marketplace. In this area too Thoreau's rebuttal to exchange embroils him in difficulties he is unable to overcome. Indeed, the two goals he sets himself as an author, to initiate civic reformation while resisting the exchange process, turn out to be so incompatible by the mid-nineteenth century as to render their attainment mutually exclusive.

Trade, Thoreau keeps insisting, "curses every thing it handles; and though you trade in messages from heaven, the whole curse of trade attaches to the business" (p. 70). Anything that is done for money, including the effort to instruct mankind, to be a "messenger from heaven" as Thoreau desires, is compromised by that very fact. Of his brief experience as a schoolteacher, he observes: "As I did not teach for the good of my fellowmen, but simply for a livelihood, this was a failure" (p. 69). In *Walden* he regularly refers to his readers as students—"Perhaps these pages are more particularly addressed to poor students," he says as early as the second paragraph (p. 4)—and he clearly sees the threat of failure hanging over his writing unless he can circumvent exchange in his dealings with his audience.

Thoreau regards life and presence, two qualities nullified by the capitalist market, as fundamental to his efficacy as an author-legislator. In censuring philanthropists, he says that their error is to distribute money rather than spending themselves. "Be sure to give the poor [i.e., poor students] the aid they most need, though it be your example which leaves them far behind" (p. 75). When he introduces himself on the first page as *Walden*'s narrator, he emphasizes his own determination to retain the "I" or the self in his writing, to speak in the first person, and he adds that he requires of every writer "a simple and sincere account of his own life, and not merely what he has heard of other men's lives" (p. 3). This conception of literature as synonymous with life and the person recurs throughout the book, for example, when Thoreau states of the written word that it "is the work of art nearest to life itself. It may be translated into every language, and not only be read but actually breathed from all human lips" (p. 102). But if words have to be alive to "inspire" the reader, there are two senses in which exchange turns them into dead letters and kills the text. Since the cost of a thing is the amount of life expended for it, the book as commodity becomes an instrument of death like any item sold on the market. It also suffers an internal demise, commodification destroying literature's "bloom" just as surely as it blights the fruits and flowers on Flint's farm.

The literary work as article of exchange and the author as tradesman was the accepted state of affairs when Thoreau wrote *Walden*. As Tocqueville noted after his visit to America, the aristocratic domain of letters had become in democratic-capitalist society "the trade of literature."[11] Thoreau, who claims to want "the flower and fruit of a man, that some fragrance be wafted from him to me, and some ripeness flavor our intercourse" (p. 77), views the situation of literary culture with dismay. The books read and written by his countrymen, he feels, are not literature at all but commodities with the impoverished nature of commodities. Singularly lacking in either fragrance or flavor, they are fit only to be consumed by "those who, like cormorants and ostriches, can digest" any sort of foodstuff (p. 104). To Thoreau, they are simply one more piece of merchandise in the unending stream of commerce which connects "the desperate city" to "the desperate country" (p. 8); and like the huckleberries transported to the Boston market from the country's hills, they lose their most essential qualities in transit. "Up comes the cotton, down goes the woven cloth; up comes the silk, down goes the woolen; up comes the books, but down goes the wit that writes them" (p. 116). Popular writers are "the machines to provide this provender," Thoreau contends, evoking his characterizations of both the huckleberry and the laboring man, and his neighbors are "the machines to read it" (p. 104–5). He proceeds to deliver a lengthy diatribe against fashionable literature and the public that devours it "with unwearied gizzard," concluding with the statement that "this sort of gingerbread is baked daily and more sedulously than pure wheat or rye-and-Indian in almost every oven, and finds a surer market" (p. 105).[12]

In addition to changing the text into a commodity and taking

away its life and essence, the marketplace endangers Thoreau's literary-
civic enterprise because it encourages the reader in his addiction to
mediation. Mediation, the substitution or replacement of one thing
or person by another, is the heart and soul of the exchange process.
In "Civil Disobedience" Thoreau disapproves of money, the medium
of exchange, on precisely the grounds that it "comes between a man
and his objects, and obtains them for him," thereby reducing his capacity for self-reliance.[13] In *Walden* he states repeatedly that he wants
the reader to obtain his objects by his own exertions (see his defini-
tion of a "*necessary of life*," p. 12). To allow the reader to accept Thoreau's experience as a substitute for his own would be the literary
equivalent of the use of money. "I would not have any one adopt *my*
mode of living on any account," he declares; rather, "I would have
each one be very careful to find out and pursue his *own way*" (p. 71).
Reading or studying something should never become a substitute for
doing it, according to Thoreau, who expresses disdain for the "common course" of instruction whereby the student (or reader) is required "to study chemistry, and not learn how his bread is made, or
mechanics, and not learn how it is earned." "'But,'" he continues,
anticipating a probable critic,

> "you do not mean that the students should go to work with
> their hands instead of their heads?" I do not mean that exactly,
> but I mean something which he might think a good deal like
> that; I mean that they should not *play* life, or *study* it merely,
> while the community supports them at this expensive game,
> but earnestly *live* it from beginning to end. How could youths
> better learn to live than by at once trying the experiment of
> living? [P. 51]

As Thoreau also points out, those who make a habit of depending on
others through exchange and the division of labor court the risk of
not being able to use their heads at all. "No doubt another *may* also
think for me; but it is not therefore desirable that he should do so to
the exclusion of my thinking for myself" (p. 46).

The reader who lets another do his thinking or his acting for him
is a reader whose consciousness has been reified. He reacts to the
words on the printed page with the same passivity and sense of non-
involvement as he feels in bowing to social reality. Most readers, in
Thoreau's view, are in exactly this position; they limit themselves to
books meant for deficient intellects and children and so "dissipate

their faculties in what is called easy reading" (p. 104). To read in this feeble way, without exerting one's mind or relying on oneself, is merely to be confirmed in one's present condition. "Easy reading," like the writing which elicits it, obviously cannot promote the spirit of independence Thoreau seeks to nurture as the author of *Walden*.

Thoreau's task as a writer-reformer accordingly requires him to make a book which is not a commodity. To spare *Walden* the fate of the huckleberry, he has to ensure that like the pond it contains "no muck" and is "too pure to have a market value" (p. 199). He also has to find some way for the reader to eliminate mediation and achieve independence in his own right. And here again Thoreau has recourse to the civic humanist ideal of husbandry for his solution. He links authorship and agriculture and portrays both the artist and his audience as figurative husbandmen, extricating *Walden* from the marketplace by means of metaphor.

In "The Bean-Field" Thoreau draws a sustained comparison between composing a text and planting a crop. He likens himself at his hoe to "a plastic artist in the dewy and crumbling sand," and he speaks of "making the yellow soil express its summer thought in bean leaves and blossoms rather than in wormwood and piper and millet grass, making the earth say beans instead of grass" (p. 156–57). The writer as metaphorical farmer remains outside the exchange process and never deals in commodities because he never sells his crop for money. His text, which never reaches the Boston market, preserves its effectiveness as a living expression of his individuality.

Thoreau also depicts the reader as a laborer "of the hands" and contrasts the toil of reading *Walden* with the "easy reading" suitable to popular literature. He claims that the diligent student who sits alone with his books throughout the day and late into the night is "at work in *his* field, and chopping in *his* woods, as the farmer is in his" (p. 136). Such strenuous intellectual exertion is the price of comprehending *Walden*, which requires a "heroic reader" to emulate its heroic author (p. 106). "The heroic books, even if printed in the character of our mother tongue, will always be in a language dead to degenerate times; and we must *laboriously* seek the meaning of each word and line, conjecturing a larger sense than common use permits out of what wisdom and valor and generosity we have" (p. 100, italics added). The reader as symbolic farmer, tasked more by *Walden*'s intricacies than by "any exercise which the customs of the day esteem" (p. 101), triumphs over mediation by having the same "laborious" experience at his desk that Thoreau has at the pond. Reading *Walden* becomes figuratively identical with being at Walden, a discipline in the mental self-reliance which enables one, or so Thoreau believes, to penetrate the "veil of reification."[14]

The qualification is in order because in metaphorizing reading and writing as activities outside history and the marketplace Thoreau disregards the realities of the text's evolution and his relation to the public. History forcibly enters *Walden* in the changes and additions made between the first draft and the published version, changes stretching over a period of nearly ten years. J. Lyndon Shanley, who has done the most thorough study of the original draft, finds that Thoreau enlarged the second half of the manuscript far more than the first, adding "more to the account of his life in the woods than to his criticism of contemporary ways," and that his major revisions were intended to emphasize the cycle of the seasons.[15] The development *within* the text, in other words, corresponds to a development *outside* the text, a shift in attitude suggesting a deepening estrangement from the social realm. Thoreau seems to have suffered a crisis of confidence in the likelihood of civic reform and the idea of his writing as a means of instigating it. Besides the addition of the "Conclusion," none of which appeared in the first draft, one change in particular is unequivocal in suggesting his disenchantment with the role of educator-legislator. In both versions he speaks of planting in his readers the seeds of sincerity, truth, and simplicity, to "see if they will not grow in this soil." But missing from the original manuscript is the sentence which comes next in the book: "Alas! I said this to myself; but now another summer is gone, and another, and another, and I am obliged to say to you, Reader, that the seeds which I planted, if indeed they *were* the seeds of those virtues, were wormeaten or had lost their vitality, and so did not come up" (p. 164).[16]

Between 1846, when he began *Walden*, and 1854, when he completed it, Thoreau had good reason to lose confidence in the viability of his civic aspirations. "Civil Disobedience" (1849) and *A Week on the Concord and Merrimack Rivers* (1849) had been published in that time; the first elicited no reaction whatsoever from the public, and the second has been described as "one of the most complete failures in literary history."[17] In the final version of *Walden* Thoreau himself alludes to the discouraging reception of his earlier work. He tells the story of an Indian who came to Concord to sell baskets but learned to his chagrin that the inhabitants did not want to buy any. The Indian wrongly supposed that he had done his part by making the baskets, "and then it would be the white man's to buy them. He had not discovered," comments Thoreau,

> that it was necessary for him to make it worth the other's while to buy them, or at least make him think that it was so, or to make something else which it would be worth his while to buy. I too had woven a kind of basket of delicate texture, but I had not made it worth any one's while to buy them. Yet not the less, in my case, did I think it worth my while to weave them, and instead of studying how to make it worth men's while to buy my baskets, I studied rather how to avoid the necessity of selling them. [P. 19]

The "kind of basket" woven by Thoreau prior to *Walden* was of course *A Week*, a book which sold so poorly, as he reveals in a journal entry for 1853, that he was obliged to take possession of "706 copies out of an edition of 1000." He confides to the journal, and the bravado does not hide his own feelings of hurt and vexation, "I believe that this result is more inspiring and better for me than if a thousand had bought my wares. It affects my privacy less and leaves me freer." [18]

Under the market system, there is no way for an author to exert influence to a significant degree without attracting a popular audience. If a book never reaches Boston, it is not likely to have much impact there. The influential writers praised by Thoreau enjoyed an "advantage" that was unavailable to him in the United States in the middle of the nineteenth century: the advantage of patronage by kings, noblemen, and warriors. Thoreau is caught in a contradiction of his own and history's devising: while he craves the authority of a founder, he refuses to view his text as a commodity and to accept "the necessity of selling" it. The failures of "Civil Disobedience" and *A Week* strengthen his antimarket resolution, but at the same time they force him to retreat from his ambition to reform the polity. Since he cannot shape popular opinion without large sales, he effectively abandons his civic project by striving to make *Walden* a difficult text at which the reader has to labor—hence a text which is inaccessible to the great majority of the public. "It is a ridiculous demand which England and America make," he writes in the "Conclusion," "that you shall speak so that they can understand you." And he goes on to voice defiant satisfaction that his own pages "admit of more than one interpretation," approximating the obscurity of the Walden ice (pp. 324–25). At this point Thoreau's celebration of figurative husbandry has become indistinguishable from the modernist credo of textual complexity, even incomprehensibility. The first draft of *Walden* was "Addressed to my Townsmen," but the last, colored by disappointment, seeks to exclude the many and narrow its appeal to a "fit audience, though few." [19]

Thoreau worked five years longer on *Walden* than he had originally intended. Expecting a success with his first book, he hoped to bring out the second as early as 1849; copies of *A Week* included the announcement that *Walden* would be published shortly. [20] But when it became evident that *A Week* was not selling, his publishers refused to issue *Walden*, and Thoreau spent five additional years revising and refining it. Since neither *A Week* nor the first draft of *Walden* is a masterpiece, this brief account of Thoreau's publishing difficulties suggests some final ironies of history. Insofar as *Walden* does "transcend" the age of Jackson, does rise above its historical moment as a consequence of its excellence as an artwork, it does so precisely because of the particular nineteenth-century circumstances under which it reached print. Its transcendence of history is rooted in the conditions of its production—its *belated* production—as a commodity to be marketed by publishers. And still more: there is the additional irony that *Walden* is its own most effective reply to Thoreau's denigrations of commercial enterprise. One need not even point out that the values of brotherhood and love, values conspicuously absent from *Walden*, are inextricably bound up with the principle of "exchange." On strictly aesthetic grounds, the text disputes the contention that "trade curses every thing it handles." Far from impairing the quality of *Walden*, commercial considerations conspired to make it a better work. *Walden* is the one undeniably great book Thoreau ever wrote, thanks in part to the operations of the marketplace.

3

Hawthorne, Melville, and the Democratic Public

The following chapter focuses on two works, both dating from the mid-nineteenth century, which examine the rewards and difficulties of writing for the literary marketplace. The first work in order of publication is "Rappaccini's Daughter," but the one I shall consider first is "Hawthorne and His Mosses," Melville's tribute to Hawthorne as the figure in whom American literature has come of age. I begin with the Melville piece because it deals openly with the situation of the American writer and provides categories which prove useful in considering Hawthorne's fiction. Melville's review has the merit of exhibiting with unusual clarity the opposition between his democratic convictions and his need to write for the democratic public—between the radically egalitarian "message" of his art and the complicated and inaccessible codes in which he feels obliged to express that message. In addition, it highlights the disparity between what might be called an artisanal and a working-class attitude toward the product of his labor. On the one side, Melville views the writer as entering into an intimate fellowship with his audience, speaking to them and for them directly in his work. On the other, he regards the writer as a kind of alienated worker, turning out texts from which his individuality has been erased—like a copyist, for example, or a girl tending a machine in a factory. Thus the "Mosses" essay points not only toward the productive tensions of *Moby-Dick* but also toward the despair and even enmity which mark such later fictions as "Bartleby, the Scrivener," "The Paradise of Bachelors and the Tartarus of Maids," and *The Confidence-Man*.

The choice of "Rappaccini's Daughter" as an illustration of Hawthorne's feelings about the marketplace requires some words of explanation. Although the story has elicited multiple interpretations, little if anything in its manifest content suggests a preoccupation with either commerce or writing. Money is mentioned only once in the tale, when Lisabetta extracts a piece of gold from Giovanni in exchange for showing him the secret entrance to Rappaccini's garden. Creation (and its ambiguities) is an obvious theme, but Doctor Rappaccini, the man responsible for the singular garden, is more commonly taken to be a misguided scientist than an artist figure. Besides the mad scientist reading, two other ways of looking at the story have been influential. One, the Christian or neo-orthodox approach, sees Beatrice as embodying the paradox of the Fortunate Fall, a creature of both sin and redemption; the second, a psychological reading, emphasizes the heroine's sexuality and Giovanni's ambivalent reaction to it. Nina Baym has summed up the critical consensus by pronouncing the story "an allegory of faith, an allegory of science, and an allegory of sex all at once."[1]

"Rappaccini's Daughter" is all of these things, but it is something more as well. The story is a fictionalized version of Hawthorne's literary circumstances in 1844 and an allegory of the common reader's inability to read him rightly. Eighteen forty-four was a year when Hawthorne was experiencing mounting frustration with the public's misunderstanding of and consequent hostility to his fiction. He turned obsessively to the problem of the writer in an unappreciative world: "The Artist of the Beautiful" and "Drowne's Wooden Image," both of which center upon the artist's struggles, were published within months of "Rappaccini's Daughter." The tale of Beatrice and her destroyers may hardly seem to belong in this company, but one of its principal themes is precisely the discrepancy between outward appearance and interior meaning. Moreover, the manifest subject of the story is more relevant than one might suppose to a major source of its inspiration, Hawthorne's pressing concern with the economics of authorship. For the Hawthorne of 1844, vainly trying to live by his pen, the poison in the garden of creation was not so much science, or disbelief, or female sexuality, as it was his difficulty in selling. And this homology between the surface of "Rappaccini's Daughter" and its deeper content leads to a more ambitious generalization: the poisonous plant in the American garden, "the Eden of the present world," (p. 96),[2] is nothing less than the growth of capitalism.

II

Reflections on literature and the marketplace were frequent and frequently impassioned in the era of American romanticism. What gave such statements their urgency, even stridency, was the widespread feeling that the value of democracy was implicated in the fate of literature as a commodity. Tocqueville's view of the matter, as set forth in the second volume of *Democracy in America*, expressed the thinking of those who looked critically, or at least skeptically, upon the economic and political tendencies of the nineteenth century. An aristocratic or patronage society, said Tocqueville, is fundamentally resistant to the commercialization of letters. Readers in aristocracies are discriminating and few in number, hence in order to succeed a writer has to satisfy the taste of a cultivated minority. He has little prospect of enriching himself and can win recognition only through great talent and exertion. Democracy, on the other hand, "introduces a trading spirit into literature." Because readers in democratic nations are numerous and easy to please, a writer of modest ability can obtain fame and considerable wealth by appealing to the judgment of the many. "Democratic literature is always infested with a tribe of writers who look upon letters as a mere trade; and for some few great authors who adorn it, you may reckon thousands of idea-mongers."[3]

The notion that commerce and majority rule are fatal to culture was already a commonplace when Tocqueville published his remarks; it did not go unchallenged in antebellum America. A characteristic rebuttal had appeared three years earlier in the July 1837 issue of the New York literary journal, the *Knickerbocker*. Systematically disputing the supposed inferiority of popular taste, an article entitled "Liberty vs. Literature and the Fine Arts" undertook to demolish the erroneous opposition indicated by its title. According to the anonymous author of the piece, a free people constitutes the best possible audience for a writer or painter of merit. This is so not because the many lack critical standards and are easily satisfied but rather because their judgment is necessarily less narrow and capricious than that of the few or an individual patron: their very numbers ensure greater tolerance and objectivity. The "people's patronage" confers two benefits upon the artist, one psychological and the other economic. It frees him from the humiliation of dependency on any one person, so that he need not live in fear of giving offense to "the master who feeds and clothes him." And the sheer size of the democratic audience, the variety of its expectations and desires, amounts to a virtual guarantee that the artist's efforts will be appreciated and liberally re-warded. "Since the period when genius became emancipated from all other patronage but that of an enlightened public," boasted the *Knickerbocker*, "we hear no more of its perishing for want, or pining in hopeless obscurity." To cite the unfortunate clients of aristocracy, in contrast, "would fill a volume, and savor of the records of a parish poor-house."[4]

Since a free people shows regard for a literary man by buying his publications, the writer in a democracy has good reason to view his activity as a form of trade. The commercialization of literature leads inevitably to its professionalization, to the appearance of authors and critics for whom writing is a full-time, money-making occupation. It also leads to the proliferation of magazines like the *Knickerbocker* which provide an outlet for literary wares and help to promote book sales through reviews and essays.[5] That such developments are salu-tary for the state of letters, and ought to be applauded rather than condemned, was the argument of an article on "Amateur Authors and Small Critics" by an unknown contributor to the *United States Magazine and Democratic Review*, another literary journal founded during the antebellum period. The commodifying of mind has be-come a fact of life in the nineteenth century, this writer emphasized, and the literary man should be judged by the same standard as other people who have goods to sell. "Thoughts form the merchandise of the writer, as stuffs and wares of the trader. If the one can convert his stock into current coin as readily as the other, on the mere ground of husbandry he deserves no little credit for his skill." Those who pre-tend that authors have no interest in being well paid are actually con-tributing to the deterioration of literature, for if writings can be pro-cured for little or nothing, it will only be a matter of time before cheapness replaces merit as the object of publishers.[6]

It is axiomatic, continued the *Democratic Review*, that the qualified professional takes his work more seriously and is held in greater es-teem than the amateur. The principle "that the laborer is worthy of his hire" applies as much to the highest pursuits of the intellect as to the common employments of the body. And professionalism should be the rule among critics no less than among authors. Only people who have knowledge of literature are fit to judge it, not just anyone who happens to be accomplished in his own line of work. "The same people who talk pertly of Milton and Wordsworth, would think it absurd for a blacksmith to attempt to take a watch to pieces." Little wonder that the amateur critic, possessing neither training nor aptitude for literary appreciation, cannot distinguish "false wares" from true and applauds with equal fervor "the jewel and the mock paste."[7]

As these last remarks indicate, "Amateur Authors and Small Critics" identified (though it did not explore) a number of problems with the confident association of democracy, commodity, and literary excellence. The professionalization to which commerce leads seems potentially at odds with the egalitarianism of popular rule. Is a polity which reserves decision making for the majority compatible with the decidedly elitist (or even aristocratic) notion that some persons are more qualified than others to evaluate an author's worth? Nor is the rise of professional critics an unmixed blessing for the author himself. While the professional reader may be better informed than the amateur, he may also pose more of a threat to the writer's privacy and economic welfare. He is apt to be an extremely skilled reader, deft at penetrating an author's reserves and piecing together his character from his work (a situation which Hawthorne in particular feared).[8] And the critic for pay may become a literary authority in his own right, able to establish or destroy a writer's standing with the general public. Professionalization may have the ironic effect of reviving the power of the individual patron and placing it in the hands of the influential critic.

Moreover, if ordinary or "amateur" readers bestow immediate popularity, as the *Democratic Review* conceded, but "the worthy, fit audience, though few," give lasting reputation, the serious writer in a democracy may find himself confronted by an impossible dilemma.[9] Without a patron to maintain him, he has no choice but to market his "spiritual commodities,"[10] yet in order to earn a sufficient livelihood he may be obliged to court the common reader to the detriment of his art. He may be forced, in other words, to sacrifice one audience, the few (and with it the hope of enduring fame), to the other, the many.

"Amateur Authors and Small Critics" appeared in the July 1845 issue of the *Democratic Review*; Hawthorne's story, "Rappaccini's Daughter," had appeared there in December 1844, half a year earlier. Almost exactly five years later, in two installments of *The Literary World* for August of 1850, Melville published his review of *Mosses from an Old Manse*, the 1846 collection of tales which included "Rappaccini's Daughter." Taken together, these circumstances provide a context for the work of two celebrated American authors who were themselves profoundly affected by the problems of commodification and the democratic audience. Hawthorne, in his bizarre story of a young woman who belongs to the plant family, and Melville, in his self-reflexive essay on "Hawthorne and His Mosses," address many of the same issues raised in the pages of antebellum magazines. They ponder the writer's complicated relation to his art as an item of exchange and to an expanding reading public which is at once "the people" and an often unreceptive market for literary goods. The two novelists sense, as the magazine writers seldom do, that their most strongly held values conflict with each other and that democracy and capitalism may be as problematic for the artist as Tocqueville supposed. And they share one more circumstance: both "Rappaccini's Daughter" and "Hawthorne and His Mosses" appear under a pseudonym, Hawthorne claiming to be a Frenchman, M. de l'Aubépine, and Melville presenting himself as "a Virginian Spending July in Vermont." Each author comes before the public wearing a disguise, unwilling or unable to face in his own proper person the democratic audience that he must educate and woo in order to survive.

III

"Hawthorne and His Mosses" announces itself as an act of celebration: celebration of Hawthorne, of democracy, and of the profound spiritual affinity between the writer and his readers. It also develops a theory of the necessary conditions for truth-telling in a society where the artist has no patron other than the marketplace. This second project, leading to an idea of literature as subterfuge and absence, flatly contradicts Melville's confident assertion of literary nationalism. It rejects as impossible and undesirable his professed reason for composing the review: to foster greater appreciation of Hawthorne and his works. Melville's essay presents the paradox of acclaiming an American "Master Genius" while advocating anonymity and even alienation as the only course available to the exceptional author.

The patriotic strain in the review is most conspicuous in Melville's attacks on "literary flunkyism towards England" (p. 546) and his glorifying of Hawthorne as a distinctively American writer. The essay postulates a special relation between the man of letters and the nation. It demands recognition for those native authors who "breathe that unshackled, democratic spirit of Christianity in all things, which now takes the practical lead in this world, though at the same time led by ourselves—us Americans" (p. 546). Such authors, by carrying

"republican progressiveness into Literature" (p. 543), constitute
themselves a kind of spiritual leadership of the country. Invoking the
familiar notion of Americans as a new chosen people, Melville on
three occasions compares Hawthorne to Christ and suggests that
failure to acknowledge "the literary Shiloh of America" corresponds
to the Jewish inability to identify the Savior (p. 550). The American
people vindicate their own capacity for judging wisely when they bestow praise on their deserving writers; they prove themselves a nation of readers worthy of a democratic literature. "It is for the nation's
sake," Melville says, "and not for her authors' sake, that I would have
America be heedful of the increasing greatness among her writers.
For how great the shame, if other nations should be before her, in
crowning her heroes of the pen" (p. 545).

The bond between the American author and his readers is a reciprocal one, Melville adds. While he denies that native genius needs
patronage in order to develop, he sees audience acceptance as not
only justifying the many's wisdom but also having positive consequences for the writer's art. Recognition from the people will inspire
"grateful impulses" in the man like Hawthorne, prompting him to
"the full flower of some still greater achievement" (pp. 546–47). And
because popular support is manifested in the market, Melville concludes his essay by lamenting Hawthorne's relative obscurity and appealing for greater sales of his works. Granted, he exclaims, "that the
books of Hawthorne have sold by the five-thousand,—what does
that signify?—They should be sold by the hundred-thousand; and
read by the million; and admired by every one who is capable of Admiration" (p. 551).

These sentiments are delivered in the tones of a fervent democrat
who expects his entreaty to fall on sympathetic ears. But as the final
qualifying phrase suggests (not "every one" but "every one who is
capable of Admiration"), Melville's patriotic effusions coexist with a
deep skepticism about the mass reading public and its aptitude for
appreciating excellence. An antidemocratic side is evident throughout the essay, revealing itself in doubts about the value of popular
renown. Hawthorne, declares Melville in this vein, has suffered ne-
glect because his fictions are "too deserving of popularity to be popular" (p. 536). Even the "all-popular" Shakespeare is admired by the
multitude for the wrong reasons. What endears him to audiences is
not his profound insight into human nature but "the noise and show
of broad farce, and blood-besmeared tragedy" with which he brings

down the house (p. 547). The favorable opinion of the people is simply not an accurate reflection of an author's worth.

Melville proceeds to sketch out the ruse which he believes Hawthorne has adopted to cope with the inhospitalities of the marketplace. The stratagem supposedly enables the author of the *Mosses* to make his work acceptable to the common reader while expressing thoughts too controversial for popular consumption. Few members of the public, Melville argues, have either "time, or patience, or palate, for the spiritual truth" as it appears in a writer of genius (p. 542). Consequently, if he wishes both to tell the truth and to attract a general audience, an artist like Hawthorne has no alternative but to disguise his meanings, to be a kind of con man who deliberately encourages misunderstanding. "This Man of Mosses," Melville claims—and he constantly describes Hawthorne in the language of vegetation— "this Man of Mosses takes great delight in hoodwinking the world" (p. 548). He tries to create a false impression of himself as "a pleasant writer, with a pleasant style,—a sequestered, harmless man . . . who means no meanings" (p. 539). He has a fondness for innocuous-sounding titles like "Young Goodman Brown," titles that lead one to expect "a supplement to 'Goody Two Shoes'" when in fact the piece is "deep as Dante" in its exploration of sin (p. 549). And this mistitling is characteristic of Hawthorne's method, according to Melville: he bathes his fictions in a seductive "Indian-summer sunlight" while charging their inner core with the "power of blackness." The reader may be bewitched by Hawthorne's sunlight; he may be dazzled by "the bright gildings in the skies" built over him; "but there is the blackness of darkness beyond; and even [the] bright gildings but fringe, and play upon the edges of thunder-clouds.—In one word, the world is mistaken in this Nathaniel Hawthorne. He himself must often have smiled at its absurd misconception of him. He is immeasurably deeper than the plummet of the mere critic" (pp. 540–41).

For Melville, in short, Hawthorne is an outwardly conventional author who smuggles into his stories dark, unpopular truths. He enters into a relation with the reading public marked by distance and manipulation, not the ideal of mutual sympathy advanced by the review. Indeed, Hawthorne assumes the existence of two reading publics, a many composed of "common eyes" (p. 550) and a superior and discerning few. His writings are "directly calculated to deceive— egregiously deceive—the superficial skimmer of pages." Genuine comprehension is possible only for the "eagle-eyed reader" such as

Melville himself who can penetrate the beguiling surface of Hawthorne's works and accompany their maker into the secret regions of the heart (p. 549). For the author of the *Mosses*, the need to sell in the marketplace leads not to democracy in literature but to aristocratic exclusion of the demos.

Mystification of the wider public has its corollary in authorial removal from the text. In his discussion of Shakespeare, Melville suggests that the prohibition against freely speaking the truth requires the artist to withdraw or efface himself from what he writes. He dare not state his convictions openly or he may give offense and drive away his audience. "For in this world of lies," Melville says, "Truth is forced to fly like a scared white doe in the woodlands; and only by cunning glimpses will she reveal herself, as in Shakespeare and other masters of the great Art of Telling the Truth,—even though it be covertly, and by snatches." Shakespeare finds safety in refusing to speak in his unmediated voice, disavowing the connection between himself and his vision of the truth. He craftily insinuates through the mouths of his dark characters the things "we feel to be so terrifically true, that it were all but madness for any good man, in his own proper character, to utter, or even hint of them" (pp. 541–42).

What is involved here is not simply an escape into fiction, as a privileged space where the truth can be told with impunity.[11] Melville insists that the author has to make himself inaccessible and, by erasing or cancelling out the traces of his identity, effectively become absent from his writing. Early in the essay he expresses a wish that "all excellent books were foundlings, without father and mother, that so it might be, we could glorify them, without including their ostensible authors" (p. 536). Only if the work is orphaned, Melville believes, only if it has been severed from its parent or producer, can it provide a secure medium for truth-telling. His use of Shakespeare is very much to the point. The nineteenth-century conception of Shakespeare highlighted his impersonality or "negative capability"; as Emerson observed of the Bard in the same year as Melville's essay, "there is not a trace of egotism," or self, in all his poetry.[12] Furthermore, a playwright has the advantage over a novelist of displaying action instead of describing it. The dramatic form is predicated on the absence of the author from the scenes represented on the stage. For the novelist or essayist, comparable protection would consist in denying authorship altogether and offering one's work anonymously or under a pseudonym. Melville recommends just this policy when he asserts that "the names of all fine authors are fictitious ones" (p. 536), and he exemplifies it when he puts a false signature to his review, attributing "Hawthorne and His Mosses" to a Virginian summering in Vermont. Melville's idea that dissimulation and anonymity are essential requirements for "Telling the Truth" in literature could not be more sharply at odds with his interest in promoting Hawthorne's reputation. Accustomed, as he admitted, to viewing his own "literary affairs in a strong pecuniary light," he knew perfectly well that authors' names and personalities were important selling points with the mass democratic public.[13] Moreover, in the *Mosses* essay he acknowledges that no effort at concealment can succeed in wholly eliminating a writer from his work. Nor is this simply a matter of a handful of readers' being perceptive enough to search out the text's hidden meanings. Even someone as secretive as Hawthorne is unwilling to empty his art of all authorial presence. He invariably wants to impart an aspect of himself to what he creates:

> No man can read a fine author, and relish him to his very
> bones, while he reads, without subsequently fancying to him-
> self some ideal image of the man and his mind. And if you
> rightly look for it, you will almost always find that the author
> himself has somewhere furnished you with his own picture.
> For poets (whether in prose or verse), being painters of Na-
> ture, are like their brethren of the pencil, the true portrait-
> painters, who, in the multitude of likenesses to be sketched, do
> not invariably omit their own. . . . [P. 547]

These remarks are something more than an interpretation of Hawthorne and an indication of his ambivalence about disclosing himself to the reader. They are a revelation of Melville's own divergent impulses toward deception and transparency as ways of relating to the book-buying public. For Melville, the work of literature is not so much an outpouring of romantic genius (though there are times when he does express this attitude) as it is the product of the artist's labor, an item to be sold for money on the market. Of *Redburn* (1849) and *White-Jacket* (1850), for example, he observed that he wrote them "almost entirely for 'lucre'—by the job, as a woodsawyer saws wood."[14] Regarding the literary text as a commodity, Melville vacillates between seeing his books as affirmations of democratic community and as alienated objects expressing little or nothing of himself. He accepts concealment and estrangement as unavoidable in exchange relations yet strives to overcome them, endeavoring to restore the face-to-face intimacy of storytelling by inserting himself into the artwork and reaching out toward his audience.[15] This conflict is constitutive of his greatest fiction. The antithetical feelings about the "trade of literature" revealed by the *Mosses* essay operate powerfully to shape the structure and narrative consciousness of *Moby-Dick*, the novel Melville was working on when Hawthorne's writing captured his imagination.

Despite its insights, the essay is less reliable as an analysis of Hawthorne. It is true that the "Man of Mosses" believes his fiction to be frequently misunderstood by the ordinary reader. But he is far from imagining himself as an author of treacherous depths who tries to camouflage his complexity by willingly courting misinterpretation. "Rappaccini's Daughter" illustrates the limitations of this reading of Hawthorne. The story shows that he views the public's failure to grasp his true nature, not in the favorable light that Melville does, but as a fatal disadvantage to his career.

IV

"Rappaccini's Daughter" was composed in a period of crisis for American writers generally and Hawthorne in particular. The severe economic depression of 1837, devastating book sales, had not yet run its course, while competition from British and (in growing numbers) French reprints "drove down the retail prices of American books to the point where the literary profession was not self-supporting."[16] Of equal concern to Hawthorne was the marked increase in home-grown competition. The 1840s saw both the flowering of Transcendentalism as an indigenous literary movement and an unprecedented outpouring of sentimental romances and adventure stories by native authors.[17] Hawthorne, who had married in 1842 and had a family to support, knew from bitter personal experience the difficulty of writing for a living in this climate. His first book of short fiction, the 1837 collection of *Twice-told Tales*, had been remaindered, and sales of the enlarged 1842 edition were insufficient to cover the publisher's costs. Surprised and angered by the public's indifference, he was soon writing to a friend of his wish "that Providence would make it somewhat more plain to my apprehension how I am to earn my bread."[18]

On the surface, "Rappaccini's Daughter" reveals little of Hawthorne's dismay over his career. Only in the self-deprecating and ironic preface, which purports to introduce the American public to the writings of M. de l'Aubépine, does Hawthorne allude to his failure to attract a popular audience. He attributes Aubépine's lack of success to the fact that he occupies "an unfortunate position between the Transcendentalists . . . and the great body of pen-and-ink men who address the intellect and sympathies of the multitude." Too remote and shadowy for the general taste, yet not metaphysical enough to suit the Transcendentalists, the Frenchman "must necessarily find himself without an audience; except here and there an individual, or possibly an isolated clique" (p. 91).

Hawthorne follows this bleak assessment of Aubépine's prospects with a more detailed sketch of his peculiar literary qualities, in the course of which he acknowledges the difficulty of knowing how to read him. The Frenchman, he contends, might have gained a "greater reputation but for an inveterate love of allegory, which is apt to . . . steal away the human warmth out of his conceptions." Yet his work is not so deficient in reality as this addiction might suggest. He tends to combine elements of the two rival schools, an unworldly aspect appropriate to Transcendentalism and a human, "pen-and-ink" side that makes one "feel as if, after all, we were yet within the limits of our native earth." The reader, Hawthorne cautions, needs "precisely the proper point of view" to appreciate this mixture; otherwise, Aubépine's productions "can hardly fail to look excessively like nonsense" (pp. 91–92).

There is a close connection between these prefatory remarks and the ensuing narrative. Four persons or characters dominate the story: Beatrice Rappaccini, Giovanni Guasconti, Dr. Rappaccini, and Dr. Baglioni. Each of these figures can be compared to some aspect of Hawthorne's situation as defined by the preface: his fiction, the reading public, the Transcendentalists, and the popular writers. Giovanni is specified as a reader from the moment he appears in the text. A medical student from the south of Italy, he is said to be "not unstudied in the great poem of his country" (p. 93). This of course is a reference to Dante's *Divine Comedy*, a work similar to "Rappaccini's Daughter" in that it also features a heroine named Beatrice. Having come to Padua to continue his education, Giovanni engages lodgings which afford him an unobstructed view of Rappaccini's garden.

The garden itself bears an unmistakable resemblance to the "neutral territory" of Hawthorne's art.[19] Its appearance recalls to mind the description of Aubépine's fictions as "fantastic" and artificial in their imagery yet still taking place within the confines of the natural world (p. 92). To Giovanni, the profuse plants seem sinister as well as beautiful. Their gorgeousness strikes him as "fierce, passionate, and even *picturesque vs. not?*

unnatural" (p. 110), and he observes Rappaccini pick his way among them like "one walking among malignant influences, such as savage beasts, or deadly snakes, or evil spirits" (p. 96). But the garden presents a different aspect to Giovanni in "the light of morning." The day after his arrival, he is "surprised, and a little ashamed, to find how real and matter-of-fact an affair it proved to be," the bright rays of the sun bringing "everything within the limits of ordinary experience" (p. 98).

What about links to Paris Jardindes Plantes?

When Beatrice Rappaccini enters this garden in answer to her father's summons, she makes an impression on Giovanni much like the mysterious plants. She seems "another flower, the human sister of those vegetable ones, as beautiful as they—more beautiful than the richest of them—but still to be touched only with a glove, nor to be approached without a mask" (p. 97). As the most dazzling creation in the garden, Beatrice is intended as an allegorical representation of Hawthorne's writing. Elsewhere he repeatedly characterizes his short fictions as flowers or plants. In "The Old Manse," for instance, he says that his stories and sketches have "blossomed out like flowers in the calm summer of my heart and mind" and proceeds to offer a "bouquet" to the reader under the title, *Mosses from an Old Manse*. Reviewers of his collected writings often made the same association, most notably Longfellow in praising the second edition of *Twice-told Tales*: "His writings retain the racy flavor of the soil. They have the healthy vigor and free grace of indigenous plants."[20] Hawthorne himself added the "w" to his family name to underline its similarity to that of a delicate flower-bearing bush. In "Rappaccini's Daughter" he emphasizes his identification with Beatrice by translating his name into French and so making even more evident its meaning as a shrub or plant—*aubépine* being the French word for hawthorn tree.

key

If Giovanni corresponds to Hawthorne's reader, and Beatrice to his art, the rival physicians in the story evoke the two kinds of writers whom he characterizes in the preface as monopolizing current taste. Rappaccini is Hawthorne's fictional Transcendentalist, a remote and shadowy creator likened at the action's climax to "an artist who should spend his life in achieving a picture or a group of statuary" (p. 126). Hawthorne refers to "the spiritual or metaphysical requisitions" of the Transcendentalist class, stressing their aloofness from the "sympathies of the multitude" (p. 91); Rappaccini, with his "cold and purely intellectual aspect," is capable of "spiritual . . . love of science" but shows little feeling for the subjects of his experiments (p. 100). Baglioni contends that his adversary "cares infinitely more for science than for mankind" (p. 99), and when Rappaccini glances at Giovanni in the street, his inquisitive look betrays "merely a speculative, not a human, interest in the young man" (p. 107). Nothing about him, in short, conveys "much warmth of heart" (p. 95). Hawthorne, it is worth noting, had a similar impression of Emerson, his Concord neighbor and preeminent Transcendentalist. In "The Old Manse," after introducing Emerson as "a great original Thinker" and remarking on the "intellectual gleam diffused about his presence," he comments that "the heart of many an ordinary man had, perchance, inscriptions which he could not read."[21]

Rappaccini's competition comes from Pietro Baglioni, who is Hawthorne's "pen-and-ink man." Relations between the two physicians have been frayed by a long-standing "professional warfare," a rivalry, as Hawthorne wryly observes, which may be followed in "certain black-letter tracts on both sides, preserved in the medical department of the University of Padua" (p. 100). A friend of Giovanni's father, Baglioni is a native of the sunny south of Italy; his genial manner suggests the hypothetical "brighter man" beside whose work the fictions of Aubépine "look excessively like nonsense" (p. 92). There is nothing in the least "shadowy" or "insubstantial" about him (p. 91). On the contrary, he is portly and jovial, a man of the senses with a hearty appetite and a fondness for wine. The popular fiction of Hawthorne's day was governed by the rationalist epistemology of the Scottish Common Sense philosophers,[22] and Baglioni speaks for this tradition in rebuking Rappaccini's experiments as irresponsible if marvellous. As he assures Giovanni, his own imagination is altogether too "sober" to deceive him into imputing a spiritual element to odors (p. 118). His sobriety does not prevent his being a storyteller, however, and he proceeds to retell "Rappaccini's Daughter" from his matter-of-fact "point of view." In his version of the tale, an Indian prince

sent a beautiful woman as a present to Alexander the Great. She was as lovely as the dawn, and gorgeous as the sunset; but what especially distinguished her was a certain rich perfume in her breath. . . . Alexander, as was natural to a youthful conquerer, fell in love with this magnificent stranger. But a certain sage physician, happening to be present, discovered a terrible secret in regard to her. . . . That this lovely woman had been nourished with poisons from her birth upward, until her whole nature was so imbued with them, that she herself had become the deadliest poison in existence. Poison was her element of life. With that rich perfume of her breath, she blasted the very air. Her love would have been poison!—her embrace death! [P. 117]

Baglioni's embedded narrative is one of three renderings of Beatrice provided by the story: Hawthorne's and Rappaccini's are the others. The struggle or rivalry in the tale is for the surrogate reader's perception of her identity. Baglioni gives a one-dimensional view of her as fatal seductress, a portrait in keeping with the melodramatic preferences of popular literature. Her "*whole nature*," he insists, has been imbued with deadly poison (my italics). He instructs Giovanni to administer the antidote to Beatrice in the hope of purifying her system and returning her "within the limits of ordinary nature" (p. 119). Rappaccini, in contrast, is intent on making his daughter into a Transcendentalist work of art—a being isolated from the multitude and outside the pale of common experience. He encourages her involvement with Giovanni so that the two of them can live apart from mankind as a separate race:

My daughter, thou are no longer lonely in the world! Pluck one of those precious gems from thy sister shrub, and bid thy bridegroom wear it in his bosom. It will not harm him now! My science, and the sympathy between thee and him, have so wrought within his system, that he now stands apart from common men, as thou dost . . . from common women. Pass on, then, through the world, most dear to one another, and dreadful to all besides! [P. 127]

The third account of Beatrice, the larger narrative composed by Hawthorne, shows her to be human as well as poisonous, innocent as well as deadly. Indeed, Hawthorne does not really dispute the fact that she has been infected by her father's plants. What his narrative questions, rather, is the relationship between the poison and Beatrice's inner being. She herself admonishes Giovanni to disregard the evidence of his eyes and trust only what she says: "If true to the outward senses, still it may be false in its essence. But the words of Beatrice Rappaccini's lips are true from the depths of the heart outward. Those you may believe!" (p. 112). Hawthorne seconds these sentiments when he asserts that "there is something truer and more real, than what we can see with the eyes, and touch with the finger" (p. 120). And there are moments when Giovanni himself, rising above his doubts, seems able "to gaze through the beautiful girl's eyes into her transparent soul" (p. 112).

As Hawthorne has pointed out in the preface, an allegorical reading is necessary to comprehend his writing. Giovanni as fictional reader is asked to see through Beatrice's physical envelope and to grasp the purity of her spiritual "essence." Instead of having faith in her inner goodness, however, he decides to institute a test to establish "whether there were those dreadful peculiarities in her physical nature, which could not be supposed to exist without some corresponding monstrosity of soul" (p. 120). At this point it becomes apparent that Giovanni has failed to find "the proper point of view" from which to interpret Hawthorne's art; he could be Melville's "superficial skimmer of pages." Assuming a direct correlation between exterior and interior, vehicle and meaning, he has already concluded that a poisonous body must signify a poisonous soul. Both Hawthorne and Beatrice vehemently protest against this way of reading allegory. Scolding Giovanni for not knowing how to estimate "the pure fountain" of the heroine's heart, Hawthorne contends that "the real Beatrice was a heavenly angel" (p. 122). "Though my body be nourished with poison," Beatrice adds, "my spirit is God's creature, and craves love as its daily food" (p. 125). Her last words to the young Neapolitan reiterate the incorrectness of his interpretation: "Oh, was there not, from the first, more poison in thy nature than in mine?" (p. 127).

"Rappaccini's Daughter" insists on the discontinuity, the lack of correspondence, between the heroine's outside and her inside, her grotesque form and her unblemished spirit. Giovanni Guasconti, embodying Hawthorne's hopes for a sympathetic audience, conflates the two sides of her being and administers the antidote prepared by Baglioni. Whereupon Rappaccini's daughter expires, killed by a misreading. The competing factions which dominate the American literary scene conspire with the reader to destroy her. Trapped in "an unfortunate position between the Transcendentalists . . . and the . . . pen-and-ink men," Beatrice suffers the fate of Hawthorne's fiction: she is left "without an audience," not even an individual or "an isolated clique."

Hawthorne, then, takes a view of his work that is precisely the opposite of Melville's. According to Melville, the author of the *Mosses* seeks to disguise his blackness with a sunny exterior; his "inside," his forbidding depths, are unacceptable to the public and have to be concealed. Hawthorne believes on the contrary that his art is only outwardly gloomy; its surface is misleading, not because it is harmless, but rather because it is dark and troubling. The "power of blackness" admired by Melville is not a reliable guide to "the real Hawthorne," any more than Beatrice's poison is a valid expression of "the real Beatrice." The "real" Hawthorne is conventional, sentimental, longs to "open an intercourse with the world,"[23] and, as Beatrice explains to her father, "would fain have been loved, not feared" (p. 127). Far from inviting misunderstanding, Hawthorne presents himself as its innocent victim, a writer deprived of an audience because the public persists in mistaking his grim exterior for his inner character. What escape the attention of "the superficial skimmer of pages" are not his subterranean profundities, as Melville supposed, but his hidden shallows, the charm, humor, and love so highly esteemed by nineteenth-century readers.[24] The results for Hawthorne's popular standing remain the same: his books sell by the five thousand or even the thousand instead of the hundred thousand, and he writes on in obscurity instead of enjoying the fame and affluence to which he aspires.

Hawthorne emerges from "Rappaccini's Daughter" as an author estranged from his audience and also, in some degree, from his art. Although in the preface he expresses "a certain personal affection and sympathy" for Aubépine's way of writing (p. 92), there are clearly times in the narrative when he shares Giovanni's distrust of Beatrice and feels frustrated by his inability to compose fiction more appealing to the ordinary reader. Like Hepzibah Pyncheon in her cent-shop, his stories handicap themselves in the market by wearing an involuntary frown which keeps them from attracting customers. And Hawthorne, who genuinely admired the "brighter" style of the pen-and-ink men, would much prefer to sport a natural smile like Phoebe's. As he stated in a letter of 1863, "I wish God had given me the faculty of writing a sunshiny book."[25]

As a judgment on the general reader, "Rappaccini's Daughter" invites some final thoughts about the extent of Hawthorne's democratic loyalties. According to the preface, Aubépine published the French version of the tale in *La Revue Anti-Aristocratique*, a journal distinguished for its championing of "liberal principles and popular rights" (p. 93). Hawthorne, who regularly contributed to the *Democratic Review*, was a staunch Jacksonian, a believer in the wisdom of the common man. *The Scarlet Letter*, written some five years later, professes confidence in the ultimate magnanimity of the many. Hawthorne says there that "the public is despotic in its temper; it is capable of denying common justice, when too strenuously demanded as a right; but quite as frequently it awards more than justice, when the appeal is made, as despots love to have it made, entirely to its generosity."[26] Whatever the accuracy of this statement as a description of the public's attitude toward Hester Prynne, it can only strike one as ironic when applied retrospectively to Giovanni, who responds to Beatrice's appeal for generosity by brutally denouncing her. The hero of Baglioni's tale about the Indian maiden, it will be recalled, is Alexander the Great, the "youthful conqueror" of Greece. Hawthorne remarks of Giovanni that he had "rather a Grecian than an Italian head, with fair, regular features, and a glistening of gold among his ringlets" (p. 104), and as the young man is converted to Baglioni's conception of the narrative, he assumes the character of the Grecian tyrant. At the end he has become the very monster he accuses Beatrice of being. In Hawthorne's story, as opposed to Baglioni's, it is Alexander-Giovanni who causes death with "his venomous scorn and anger" (p. 124).

The implication of this outcome is that author-audience relations in America are deadly, even murderous, for the author. The tale pictures a common reader whose behavior is more consistent with Tocqueville's "tyranny of the majority" than Hawthorne's benign democratic despotism. It exposes the ideal of a free people as enlightened patron of the arts as a myth. Hawthorne turns out to be a democrat of a decidedly ambiguous stripe, a man who was to spend the remainder of his life trying to escape dependency on his audience, seeking one political sinecure after another rather than trust the public to buy his books. The editor of *La Revue Anti-Aristocratique*, whom he praises in the preface for defending popular rights, is identified as "the Comte de Bearhaven" (p. 93). Like the Count, Hawthorne espouses his democratic principles from the vantage point of an aristocrat who can never quite subdue his suspicions of the multitude. He is the anti-aristocrat as man of rank.

The Count and M. de l'Aubépine seem far more cynical in their dealings with the broad democratic audience than Hawthorne, at least the Hawthorne of "Rappaccini's Daughter." They exhibit a greater willingness to manipulate the common reader and to exploit the aristocratic distinction between the few and the many. The preface states that they published the story in French as *Beatrice; ou la Belle Empoisonneuse* (p. 93)—"Beatrice; or the Beautiful Poisoner." This title is more descriptive of Baglioni's one-dimensional account of the Indian princess than of the actual narrative of Beatrice Rappaccini. It nullifies the complexity of her identity. Its use recalls Melville's remarks about Hawthorne's predilection for titles designed to allure and mislead the public. Hence the French title might be said to look ahead to the Hawthorne of *The Scarlet Letter* and *The House of the Seven Gables*—a Hawthorne, as Melville argues, who conceals a subversive aspect beneath his official surface and gilds his blackness with Indian summer sunlight.

4

To Speak in the Marketplace

The Scarlet Letter

I

In the summer of 1849 Hawthorne was discharged from his post as surveyor of the Salem customhouse and forced to resume writing for a living. The prospect was not a happy one for the author of "Rappaccini's Daughter." In the five years since the first appearance of that story, there had been little improvement in Hawthorne's standing with the common reader. He remained, as Poe put it in a generally hostile review of *Mosses from an Old Manse*, "*the* example, *par excellence*, in this country, of the privately-admired and publicly-unappreciated man of genius."[1] While he certainly wished to retain the good opinion of discriminating readers, the loss of the surveyorship made it more imperative than ever that Hawthorne broaden his appeal. Poverty was a literal possibility unless he could overcome the lack of public support that had plagued his career. In fact, when his savings ran out a few months after his dismissal, he was obliged to accept charity from friends in order to maintain his family. "Ill-success in life is really and justly a matter of shame," he remarked to a correspondent at this time. "The only way in which a man can retain his self-respect, while availing himself of the generosity of his friends, is, by making it an incitement to his utmost exertions, so that he may not need their help again. I shall look upon it so,—nor will shun any drudgery that my hand shall find to do, if thereby I may win bread."[2]

The Scarlet Letter (1850) was the product of Hawthorne's urgent need to compose a bestseller. At the heart of the book lies the dilemma he confronted as someone both eager for and fearful of popular success. Basically Hawthorne had two roles available to him as an American man of letters in the mid-nineteenth century. He had the model of his own experience as a writer for a small coterie of admirers, a writer who enjoyed critical esteem as a truth-teller but who felt ashamed of his impoverishment. The alternative course, to follow the pen-and-ink men in appealing to the multitude, would presumably bring him fame and money but might require him to violate the integrity of his art. *The Scarlet Letter* is an attempt to come to terms with these apparently irreconcilable approaches toward writing for the marketplace. Hawthorne's predicament shapes the novel's characters and structure and can be discerned in the very texture of the world he creates. It also appears in the text's acknowledgment of the difficulties of its own composition. For Hawthorne, the effort to articulate a cosmos is intimately bound up with his uncertainty as an artist who has to sell but wants to speak the truth.[3]

II

The fictive world portrayed in *The Scarlet Letter* is only nominally the world of Puritan Boston. The novel presents a social environment in which seeing and being seen, observing others and being gazed at in turn, constitute the principal forms of human activity. Desire for historical accuracy no doubt contributes to this pervasive emphasis on visual processes. Hawthorne knew from his sources that the Puritans did indeed monitor each other's conduct and drag "iniquity . . . into the sunshine" (p. 54). But his imaginative construction of how people think and feel in a world of spectators, of the constant sense they have of being scrutinized, owes more to his own experience as an author than to his reading about the colonial past. He has effectively reproduced the texture of interchange in a society where observation and appearance had become all-important: the market society of Jacksonian America.[4]

For Hawthorne's main characters in particular, the condition of being scrutinized by others is the dominant fact of their lives. In the opening scene, Hester emerges from prison to encounter the assembled inhabitants of Boston, "all with their eyes intently fastened on the iron-clamped oaken door" (p. 49). Making her way to the scaffold, where she must stand before "the public gaze" (p. 55), she tries to sustain herself "under the heavy weight of a thousand unrelenting eyes, all fastened upon her, and concentrated at her bosom" (p. 57). This is what Hawthorne himself regards as most abhorrent about Hester's punishment, that she is made "the object of severe and universal observation" (p. 60) and is denied the relief of concealment: "There can be no outrage, methinks, against our common nature,—whatever be the delinquencies of the individual,—no outrage more flagrant than to forbid the culprit to hide his face for shame" (p. 55). Nor is Hester permitted to withdraw from sight after her ordeal on the scaffold. The indignity of being stared at is regularly reenacted in her daily life. Condemned to wear the scarlet letter at all times, she must "become the general symbol at which the preacher and moralist might point, and in which they might vivify and embody their images of woman's frailty and sinful passion. Thus the young and pure would be taught to look at her . . . as the figure, the body, the reality of sin" (p. 79).

Dimmesdale is more fortunate in that he escapes public censure as Hester's lover, but he too is closely watched. His professional duties require him to mount the pulpit every Sunday and "meet so many eyes turned upward to [his] face" (p. 191). Attended by Chillingworth, who lodges with him in the same house, he passes virtually his every moment "under the eye of his anxious and attached physician" (p. 125). "Never did mortal suffer what this man has suffered," Chillingworth gloats about his patient. "And all, all, in the sight of his worst enemy" (p. 171). Since even a casual glance has the power to unsettle him, Dimmesdale develops the habit of avoiding eye contact with anyone or anything: "it was the clergyman's peculiarity," Hawthorne writes, "that he seldom, now-a-days, looked straightforth at any object, whether human or inanimate" (p. 131). Neither of the lovers can find respite from unwelcome scrutiny save in the seclusion of the forest and the company of each other: "Here, seen only by his eyes, the scarlet letter need not burn into the bosom of the fallen woman! Here, seen only by her eyes, Arthur Dimmesdale, false to God and man, might be, for one moment, true!" (p. 195–96).

The sensation of being constantly looked at like Hester and Arthur is one that Hawthorne associates with the exchange process. His very title as Surveyor in the Salem customhouse reminds him of the centrality of observation in the marketplace: buyers and sellers must make accurate judgments about the reliability of an individual or the value of a piece of merchandise. Hawthorne's most explicit treatment of this subject occurs in *The House of the Seven Gables* (1851), the novel he wrote immediately after *The Scarlet Letter*. He describes Hepzibah Pyncheon's attempt to open a cent-shop and appraises the marketability of a winning exterior. The decision to enter business requires Hepzibah to come before "the public eye" and encounter "the public gaze."[5] Hawthorne emphasizes that her procrastination stems in large part from a reluctance to be stared at: "It might have been fancied . . . that she expected to minister to the wants of the community, unseen, . . . holding forth her bargains to the reverential and awe-stricken purchaser, in an invisible hand" (2:40). When she does at last assume her position behind the counter, Hepzibah is tortured "with a sense of overwhelming shame, that strange and unloving eyes should have the privilege of gazing" at her (2:46). An involuntary scowl, frightening to customers, hurts her chances of success; in a commercial and spectatorial culture, as Uncle Venner notes, appearance matters more than substance. Venner advises Hepzibah to smile as pleasantly as she possibly can when handing customers the articles they ask for. Even an inferior piece of merchandise, he assures her, will make a hit with the public if it is accompanied by "a good, warm, sunny smile" rather than her customary grimace (2:66). The exceptional fortune of Hepzibah's cousin, the Judge, proves the truth of this Benjamin Franklin–like counsel about playing to the audience. The Judge is inwardly corrupt but always wears a dazzling smile, and he has been rewarded with both wealth and respectability for his zealous cultivation of "the public eye." (The cousins are contrasted in a chapter pointedly entitled "The Scowl and Smile.")[6]

Hepzibah's experience with the cent-shop is a metaphor for Hawthorne's own entrance into the exchange process, for his own decision to use "the House of the Seven Gables as the scene of his commercial speculations" (2:36). He knows that much like his elderly shopkeeper he must meet "the public gaze" in order to sell his writings. Thus he speaks in "The Custom-House" of his intention to bring *The Scarlet Letter* "before the public eye" (p. 34). As with all sellers of commodities, there are two aspects to this encounter with potential customers. Not only must Hawthorne induce the reader to adopt "precisely the proper point of view" from which to construe his narratives (as he phrased it in the preface to "Rappaccini's Daughter"), he must figuratively place himself before the reader's gaze and attempt to satisfy his curiosity. In the introductions to both *The Scarlet Letter* and the *Mosses* collection, he greets the public at the threshold of his fiction and provides an extended conversational account of his personal circumstances. Temperamentally a shy man, he seems almost as uncomfortable about confronting the scrutiny of an audience as Hepzibah behind the counter or Hester on her pedestal of shame. "So far as I am a man of really individual attributes," he insists in "The Old Manse,"[7] "I veil my face," and in "The Custom-House" he announces his determination to "keep the inmost Me behind its veil" (p. 4).

Yet Hawthorne realizes that far from shunning "the great Eye of the Public,"[8] he must try to make a favorable impression on it to succeed as an author. He must come forward, as the beadle says to Hester, and "show [his] scarlet letter in the market-place" (p. 54). In this respect Hawthorne's situation is closely analogous to that of his Puritan heroine and her pastor. Hester makes her initial appearance in the chapter entitled "The Market-Place," and it is there, in "the rude market-place of the Puritan settlement," that she is forced to stand as a "spectacle" for the multitude to gaze at (pp. 56–58). Dimmesdale first braves "the eyes of the whole crowd" in the same location, when he calls upon Hester to confess (p. 66), and he returns there for his final speech to the people of New England, the "silent and inactive spectators" of his dying moments (p. 253). This is the situation of all persons in commercial society: they must enter the marketplace and submit themselves to the scrutiny and evaluation of others.[9]

Hawthorne's use of the marketplace of a precapitalist settlement to explore his own status as professional author requires explanation. To the modern reader, the scaffold of a seventeenth-century Bible commonwealth may seem the antithesis of the mass market of the antebellum era. One involves face-to-face contacts, the other depersonalized relations of exchange mediated by money. Yet obviously the distinction between the two realms did not appear so firm to Hawthorne—nor was it in actuality. Though the capitalist marketplace drew a line between the public and the private, it also blurred the demarcation. The writer wishing to sell had to publicize himself, and he had to try to gratify the desire of his remote audience to know as much as possible about him. The public domain was always menacing the barriers Hawthorne erected to protect his private being. As he keeps saying in his prefaces, the figure who steps forth to converse with the reader is not the real, inner man; but he could not feel confident that the self exhibited in his art was secure from invasive inquiry. The vulnerability to exposure of the secret self is an overriding concern in *The Scarlet Letter*, and Hawthorne's eventual way of dealing with the problem, the demise or disappearance of the writer, prefigures one of the leading techniques of modernism.

What is perhaps most striking about the opening tableau of *The Scarlet Letter* is the contrast between the actions of Hester and the minister as they stand exposed before the Puritan spectators. Called upon to confess, to divulge the secrets of her heart in public, Hester shakes her head and declares in a firm voice, "I will not speak!" (p. 68). Her defiant attitude is the opposite of Arthur's. He is also summoned to speak in the marketplace, and despite the false position in which this places him, he delivers a moving speech charging Hester to make known the identity of her child's father. A remarkably effective orator, Dimmesdale enjoys great power over his audience. Hawthorne reports that his voice was so tremulously rich and sweet that it vibrated "within all hearts, and brought the listeners into one accord of sympathy" (p. 67).

The difference in status and behavior of Hawthorne's principal characters dramatizes the conflict in his mind between two radically opposed conceptions of the artist's role and relation to the public. On one side is the version of the artist represented by Hester, a scorned outcast who makes no compromises with her audience and is indifferent to its approval. If she cannot speak the truth in the marketplace, she will not speak there at all. As she cautions Pearl after their interview with Arthur in the woods, "We must not . . . talk in the market-place of what happens to us in the forest" (p. 240). Dimmesdale, who embodies the other side of Hawthorne's thinking, is a type of the artist for whom fame and popularity are everything. Even though his conscience revolts "at the contrast between what I seem and what I am" (p. 191), he is willing to conform to the expectations of his audience in order to obtain and hold their admiration. In contrast to Hester, of whom Hawthorne says, "infamy was babbling around her in the market-place" (p. 118), Dimmesdale stands "at the head of the social system" and commands the veneration of the populace (p. 200). Hawthorne notes that after he delivers the Election Sermon, "The street and the market-place absolutely babbled, from side to side, with applauses of the minister" (p. 248).

III

The Scarlet Letter is a book preoccupied with the acts of speaking and writing.[10] Letters, words, and sentences all have a prominent place in the plot. The title itself refers to the letter A, the first letter in the alphabet and thus the start of written expression. The entire New England community is anxious to know the name Hester refuses to speak on the scaffold, the one word or two that will reveal her lover. At the end of the novel Hawthorne proposes to condense its moral into a single sentence (in fact, he requires four), and the last line is "a herald's wording . . . which might serve for a motto and description of our now concluded legend" (p. 264). Moreover, the book's action is almost entirely verbal, consisting of speeches, sermons, conversations, and interior monologues. It even begins with an account of how it came into being, the story of Hawthorne's discovery of the manuscript supposedly belonging to Mr. Surveyor Pue.

Within the narrative proper, the difficulty or problematic nature of communication is far more typical than verbal facility. Hester's resistance to speaking in the marketplace establishes the pattern. Characters, the minister included, refuse to speak or are sworn to silence, and things are frequently misnamed or not named rather than permitted access to utterance. Just as Dimmesdale fails to come forward and name himself as Hester's lover, so Chillingworth assumes a false name to conceal his identity as her husband. When he first sees Hester on the scaffold, the physician places his finger on his lips and signals her not to acknowledge him. "Recognize me not, by word, by sign, by look!" he commands her during the interview in prison (p. 76). The principal actors take to expressing themselves through gesture, as though language were inadequate as well as inadvisable. Dimmesdale lacks the courage to admit his share in Hester's sin, but he keeps his hand over his breast as a kind of physical substitute for spoken confession. Chillingworth also communicates his state of mind through his body, his shoulder becoming more and more misshapen as his deformity of spirit worsens. And Hester vents her defiance of Puritan mores in her silence and her sewing. She embroiders the scarlet letter with a "luxuriance of fancy" that goes "greatly beyond what was allowed by the sumptuary regulations of the colony" (p. 53).

The people in Hawthorne's Boston have trouble grasping each other's meaning and making themselves understood. Dimmesdale voices a common complaint when he remarks to Chillingworth, "You speak in riddles, learned Sir" (p. 135). Pearl, who has a particularly trying time with language, seems to represent Hester's inarticulation intensified. On the night of the vigil, she presses her lips to Dimmesdale's ear and, "in a tongue unknown to the erudite clergyman," whispers a stream of gibberish that "did but increase the bewilderment of his mind" (p. 156). Elsewhere she utters "incoherent exclamations" (p. 94), and when Hester tosses away the letter, she reacts not with words but with "a fit of passion," mystifying her parents with her "piercing shrieks" and "extravagant contortions"

(p. 210). The extraordinary number of unanswered questions is another indication of how hard it is for communication to occur. Chilling-worth asks about Dimmesdale, "Who is he?" (p. 75); Dimmesdale makes the same inquiry about Chillingworth, "Who is that man, Hester?" (p. 156); and Pearl nags her mother with endless questions ranging from "What does the scarlet letter mean?" to "Why does the minister keep his hand over his heart?" (p. 181). Hawthorne sums up the baffled quality of verbal interchange in the book by commenting on "how long a time often passes before words embody things" (p. 224).

The difficulty of communication among Hawthorne's characters is matched by his own hesitation about speaking to the public. His prefatory note and his writing style reveal his empathy with Hester's refusal to disclose herself in the marketplace. Few other works by a major American author are so full of doubts and apologies for their existence. At the outset of "The Custom-House," Hawthorne deplores his autobiographical impulse and insists that he will withhold as much information as he divulges. "It is scarcely decorous . . . to speak all," he says, "even where we speak impersonally" (p. 4). The reader of the introductory sketch discovers that it has been a struggle for him to speak at all. The sketch is the chronicle of a writing block, describing Hawthorne's problems in composing the romance. He simply could not bring his imaginative faculty to life while serving in the customhouse, where the distraction of daily affairs prevented him from transporting himself into a different age. "I had ceased to be a writer of tolerably poor tales and essays," he laments of his three years in government, "and had become a tolerably good Surveyor of the Customs" (p. 38).

The constraints on utterance of which Hawthorne complains in the preface continue to affect his style in the romance. He shows as much reluctance as his characters to speak the name of certain things: one word he makes a point of never mentioning is "adultery." A habit of indirect speech establishes itself from the beginning, as Hawthorne typically notifies the reader of an important discourse or exchange but then, instead of providing a literal transcription, offers nothing more detailed than a summary. Of the sermon delivered by the Reverend Mr. Wilson, the reader is told only that it dwelt upon sin, "with continual reference to the ignominious letter" (p. 68). Hawthorne writes at the critical moment of the forest scene, "Then, all was spoken!" (p. 198), but all the reader learns of what was said is that Hester and Arthur resolved to flee to Europe on the day after the Election Sermon. And the Election Sermon itself is not included in the book, merely its "subject" in a highly ambiguous one-paragraph synopsis.

Even when Hawthorne describes an exchange or occurrence directly, he makes the reader aware of the inhibitions that hamper his speech. His scruples about saying something in a forthright manner are apparent in his use of phrases such as "nay, why should we not speak it?" (p. 193), "we hesitate to reveal" (p. 215), and "we blush to tell it" (p. 220). He has a tendency to correct or rephrase his previous statements, as in the many constructions based on "or, rather": "a fanciful, or, we might rather say, a fantastic ingenuity" (p. 83); "his brother clergyman,—or, to speak more accurately, his professional father" (p. 150); "this sorely tempted, or—shall we not rather say?—this lost and desperate man" (p. 219).

Hawthorne's reluctance to commit himself in language causes him to avoid affirmative statements and to pose as many questions to his audience as his characters address to each other. The entire text is an interrogative, demanding to know, "what does the scarlet letter mean?" Within the text, Hawthorne importunes the reader with questions that vary from the self-evident to the unanswerable. "Had Hester sinned alone?" (p. 86), he wonders about his heroine, and he asks, "What did it betoken?" (p. 177), when she persists in hating Roger Chillingworth for having married her. A single "what?" may occur in the midst of a sentence ("The very first thing which [Pearl] had noticed, in her life, was—what?—not the mother's smile . . ." [p. 96]), or a sentence may consist wholly of questions ("Then, what was he?—a substance?—or the dimmest of shadows?" [p. 143]). The minister's night on the scaffold elicits a battery of questions ("Why, then, had he come hither? Was it but the mockery of penitence?" [p. 148]), and at times the questions seem to run on interminably, as when a sequence of seven concludes the first paragraph of chapter 15, "Hester and Pearl."

The note of questioning in *The Scarlet Letter* is also discernible in Hawthorne's choice of individual words. One detects an agonizing over language, a struggle to find the appropriate terms in which to render experience. Hester sees in Pearl's face "a look so intelligent, yet inexplicable, so perverse, sometimes so malicious, but . . . accompanied by a wild flow of spirits" (p. 92); and her own face in the prison interview registers "a slow, earnest look . . . , not precisely a look of fear, yet full of doubt and questioning" (pp. 72–73). *The Scarlet Letter* is remarkable for the incidence of words like "inexpressible" that proclaim the inadequacy of language to the task of representation. Misery is "unspeakable" (p. 145), solace and torment "unutterable" (p. 132), horror "nameless" (p. 156), breath "inarticulate" (p. 124), and the games of a child "inexpressibly sad" (p. 95). Hawthorne's use of such terms furnishes a perfect illustration of his own statement about how often words fall short of embodying the things they describe.

The larger unit of sentences reveals a similar tentativeness to Hawthorne's prose. He has an unusual habit of repeating words or phrases verbatim within a sentence. This kind of writing stutter occurs so often that it amounts to a stylistic signature. The pattern first appears in the preface ("I seem to have a stronger claim . . . a stronger claim . . ." [p. 91]), can be found at numerous places throughout the story ("It may seem marvellous, that, with the world before her, . . . it may seem marvellous . . ." [p. 79]), and continues to the very end ("She had returned, therefore, and resumed . . . resumed the symbol . . ." [p. 263]). Hawthorne's repeated circling back to words used but a moment before suggests a reluctance to go on, to progress in the sentence. It is as though moving the narrative forward requires a greater effort than he can muster.

The linguistic inhibition felt everywhere in *The Scarlet Letter* rests on a paradox—the paradox that the text is Hawthorne's first major novel. What was originally conceived as a story of modest length expanded in a few short months into the longest fiction he had written. According to his wife Sophia, he spent nine hours a day at his desk, twice his normal allotment, and he wrote "*immensely*" with an ease and confidence which he was never again to equal.[11] A book that endlessly protests how hard it was to write actually required less than six months to complete. While the doubts and reservations are certainly real, they are no more so than the furious pace of composition. The split embodied in the figures of Hester and Arthur is reenacted in the production of the novel as well as in its prose. Like the minister, Hawthorne speaks in the marketplace with eloquence and power, but like his feminine protagonist he keeps remonstrating against the ordeal of having to speak there.

IV

The conflict illustrated by the opening pages of *The Scarlet Letter* is a major theme in "The Custom-House" and elsewhere in Hawthorne's writings. His ambivalence frequently issues in a pretense that he is content to address a small circle of friends rather than the general reader, whose "unkindly eyes" might happen to "skim over what was never meant for them."[12] In the very first paragraph of "The Custom-House," Hawthorne discriminates between "the many who will fling aside his volume, or never take it up," and "the few who will understand him, better than most of his schoolmates and life-mates" (p. 3). This pose of literary innocence has roots in the eighteenth-century ideal of the author as a cultivated gentleman for whom writing is a sideline, not a profession. The respectable man of letters supposedly never wrote for money, published anonymously if he deigned to publish at all, and addressed his work to a select group of peers.[13] Hawthorne, whose own early tales appeared without his name and whose reclusiveness reinforced the appeal of anonymity, is wrapping himself in this tradition when he downplays the commercial aspects of his fiction. The self-portrait he gives in "The Custom-House" is of a harmless "idler" whose literary efforts are more embarrassing than lucrative. He imagines his hard-headed ancestors deriding him for being "a writer of story-books" (p. 10), and he professes to garner satisfaction from the "good lesson" that his dreams of fame and fortune have come to nothing (p. 26).

But there is another Hawthorne in "The Custom-House," a shrewd professional who writes for money and reacts to his dismissal from the surveyorship by "making an investment in ink, paper, and steel-pens" (p. 43). This Hawthorne imagines Mr. Surveyor Pue, his ancient predecessor, exhorting him to bring the story of Hester Prynne "before the public" with the admonition, "do this, and the profit shall be all your own! You will shortly need it, for it is not in your days as it was in mine, when a man's office was a life-lease, and oftentimes an heirloom" (p. 33). The practical Hawthorne has no illusions about his position as a dealer in commodities of the mind. He even develops a wry equation between the writer's fictions and the trader's merchandise. Although his name was no longer "blazoned abroad on title-pages" during his term in office, he was amused to find that it had "another kind of vogue. The Custom-House marker imprinted it, . . . on pepper-bags, and baskets of anatto, and cigar-boxes, and bales of all kinds of dutiable merchandise, in testimony that those commodities had paid the impost." Such was the "queer vehicle of fame" by which "a knowledge of [his] existence" was disseminated (p. 27).

As a penurious author hoping to attract a national audience, Hawthorne is in fact a "man of traffic" much like the Salem merchants

(p. 44). He cannot maintain the fiction of gentlemanly amateur speaking to his friends. The gentlemanly ideal was essentially British and aristocratic, resting on the practice of patronage, and Hawthorne was well aware of its inappropriateness to a democratic market culture. If he wrote for a "few," they were professional men of letters like himself, reviewers and critics for the leading journals of the antebellum era. His real interest was in persuading the "many" to buy his books. By writing the introductory sketch, he demonstrated a sound business sense aimed at capitalizing on the public's curiosity about his dismissal. Despite his disclaimer, he surely anticipated that the sketch would create "an unprecedented excitement in the respectable community around him," as he reports in the prefatory note to the second edition (p. 1).

Unbosoming in the marketplace, speaking openly there of one's private circumstances, was a widely acknowledged requirement for popular success. In the nascent art of promotion, as William Charvat has pointed out, "authors' names were brand names" and "reticences were doomed."[14] Great men of letters have been "egotists all—a sad race of talkers about themselves," affirmed Evert A. Duyckinck in the May 1845 issue of the *Democratic Review*. Yet even the most avid candidate for literary reputation was not half so industrious in self-promotion as the ordinary tradesman, with his advertisements, placards, and "name on every packing box." To the accusation that "the author is making a trade and merchandize of all that a man should hold most dear and secret," Duyckinck replied: "The merchant seeks notoriety for the same ends, and as nearly as he can, with the same means, as the author." Duyckinck was strongly in favor of such intimate disclosure and called for ever more exhibition of "personality" in literature. What is wanted, he said, is insight into "the peculiar secret principle" of a writer's genius, precisely the kind of personal information "which is not to be picked up on the highway."[15]

Hawthorne similarly states that it is "within the law of literary propriety" to address the public in his own person and chat of his experience in the customhouse (p. 27). He craves a human connection to his readers, but he hardly shares Duyckinck's enthusiasm for self-exposure. On the contrary, he resents this concession to the marketplace, though recognizing its necessity, and cannot conceal his discomfort about opening himself to even the most supposedly sympathetic of readers. His desire for "some true relation with his audience" does not prevent him from veiling his "inmost Me" from the reader's eye and declining to indulge in "confidential depths of revelation." He even disguises himself as an editor, offering this hoary and patently artificial convention as his "true reason for assuming a personal relation with the public" (pp. 3–4).

Hawthorne's double attitude toward self-disclosure is equally marked in other prefaces, most notably "The Old Manse."[16] He invites the reader of this autobiographical sketch to be a "guest" in his home but denies having told him any but the most general of confidences (10:6).

> Has the reader gone wandering, hand in hand with me,
> through the inner passages of my being, and have we groped
> together into all its chambers, and examined their treasures or
> their rubbish? Not so. We have been standing on the green
> sward, but just within the cavern's mouth, where the common
> sunshine is free to penetrate, and where every footstep is there-
> fore free to come. [10:32]

In a tone of defiance that suggests his Puritan heroine, Hawthorne then goes on to insist that he is not "one of those supremely hospitable people, who serve up their own hearts delicately fried, with brain-sauce, as a tidbit for their beloved public" (10:33). By the end of the sketch it is difficult to ascertain whether the "honored reader" (10:32) is his friend or foe. Hawthorne pictures himself ushering the reader into his study and entreating his attention to the tales that follow. Whereupon he abruptly changes his tone and declares that this ostensibly cordial gesture is actually "an act of personal inhospitality . . . which I was never guilty of, nor ever will be, even to my worst enemy" (10:35).[17]

The friendly reader who looks remarkably like an adversary is also the subject of a letter Hawthorne wrote to his publisher, James T. Fields, while he was completing *The Scarlet Letter*. Afraid that the romance proper would appear too gloomy "to the reader's eye," he urged Fields to publish it in a volume composed of several tales:

> A hunter loads his gun with a bullet and several buckshot, and
> following his sagacious example, it was my purpose to conjoin
> the one long story with half a dozen shorter ones; so that,
> failing to kill the public outright with my biggest and heaviest
> lump of lead, I might have other chances with the smaller bits.

Besides "shooting" the reader, whom he persisted in calling his guest, Hawthorne was not above advising Fields on a promotional scheme to entrap unwary purchasers. In the same letter he recommended printing the book's title page in red ink; though unsure about "the good taste of so doing," he thought the idea would prove "attractive to the great gull whom we are endeavoring to circumvent."[18]

Hawthorne felt hostility toward the reading public for the same reason that he was so ready to exploit it, because he doubted his natural ability to satisfy the popular taste. In "The Custom-House" he tries to convey the impression that he welcomed his removal from office and gladly exchanged the patronage of Uncle Sam for the challenge of competing in the literary marketplace. In reality, he campaigned actively for reinstatement and never ceased in his efforts to return to government employment, hoping to find there the security that kept eluding him as an author.[19] Yet Hawthorne's desire to succeed at the trade of literature was as genuine—and in 1849, as pressing—as his apprehensions about the possibility. The opposing impulses that prompted him both to defy his audience and to seek its approval, to feign indifference to fame or profit and to discuss his private affairs in public, receive articulation in *The Scarlet Letter* not only through the book's characters and style but in its very structure. Openness is paired with concealment and removal from the reader, "The Custom-House" with the romance proper, the "I" who unburdens himself with the impersonal narrator who relates the history of Hester and the minister. And underlying this duplex structure is an ironic reversal. The autobiographical sketch, hedged about with reticences and outright falsehoods, conceals its author and refuses intimacy. The ensuing romance, with its seeming impersonality, lays bare the motives behind Hawthorne's linguistic hesitancy and air of furtiveness toward the reader.

V

After her humiliation in the marketplace, Hester settles into an existence on the margins of the Puritan community—an existence much like that of her creator during his protracted literary apprenticeship. Hawthorne remembered those years as a time when he worked in seclusion and obscurity and met with a "total lack of sympathy from the public."[20] Hester experiences a similar isolation as the wearer of the scarlet letter. "In all her intercourse with society," Hawthorne writes, ". . . there was nothing that made her feel as if she belonged to it" (p. 84), the letter having removed her from "ordinary relations with humanity" and enclosed her "in a sphere by herself" (p. 54). Far from pursuing wealth or eminence, she shuns the public eye and relinquishes "even the humblest title to share in the world's privileges" (p. 160). She desires nothing "beyond a subsistence" (p. 83) and is content to "earn daily bread for little Pearl and herself by the faithful labor of her hands" (p. 160).

Hester's situation suggests the benefits as well as disadvantages to being "the outcast of society" (p. 161). She is the first full-length representation in American literature of the alienated modern artist, a figure Hawthorne finds both admirable and misguided. Despite her apparent conformity, she remains a rebel; her needlework and her silence are gestures of resistance. And despite the "inquisitorial watch" kept over her by the magistrates (p. 81), she develops into a fearless and self-reliant thinker. "Alone, as to any dependence on society," she assumes "a freedom of speculation, then common enough on the other side of the Atlantic, but which our forefathers, had they known of it, would have held to be a deadlier crime than that stigmatized by the scarlet letter" (p. 164). Hawthorne is not uncritical of "such latitude of speculation" and contends that Hester's solitude has "taught her much amiss" (pp. 199–200). But he portrays her as an apostle of liberty who preserves her freedom of mind because she has "no hope, and seemingly no wish, of gaining any thing" from society (p. 160).

Besides Hawthorne himself, who was enough of a maverick to have spent a year at Brook Farm, there is another nineteenth-century American thinker whom Hester resembles: Henry D. Thoreau. Although in "The Custom-House" Hawthorne refers to his iconoclastic former neighbor only in passing, mentioning him "in his hermitage at Walden" (p. 25), relations between the two men were fairly extensive, and Thoreau may well have been in his mind when he wrote *The Scarlet Letter*. "Civil Disobedience" had been published in 1849 in a miscellany edited by Elizabeth Peabody, Hawthorne's sister-in-law, and Hawthorne was familiar with both *A Week* and the early versions of *Walden*, having arranged for Thoreau to lecture at the Salem Lyceum on his experiment in the woods. He found Thoreau exasperating but admired his integrity and independence of thought. "He is an upright, conscientious, and courageous man," Hawthorne observed of him several years later. "Still, he is not an agreeable person; and in his presence one feels ashamed of having any money, or a house to live in, or so much as two coats to wear, or of having written a book that the public will read—his own mode of life being so

unsparing a criticism on all other modes, such as the world approves."
To Hawthorne, Thoreau was "a true man" who had rejected the rewards but also the compromises of conforming to the marketplace.[21]

Hester Prynne is similarly devoted to the truth, and she too does her speaking in the woods rather than "the market-place of Boston" (p. 230). "In all things . . . , I have striven to be true!" she exclaims to Arthur. "Truth was the one virtue which I might have held fast, and did hold fast through all extremity" (p. 193). Dimmesdale, "the untrue man" (p. 145), thoroughly dominates speech in public settings like the marketplace and the Governor's residence. In the scene dealing with Pearl's upbringing, Hester beseeches him to intervene for her with the Puritan elders: "Speak thou for me! Thou wast my pastor. . . . Speak for me!" (p. 113). But in the forest, Hester's voice is the one that carries authority. Dimmesdale is out of his element and pleads with her, "Advise me what to do" (p. 196). The wilderness is the setting where Hester, like Thoreau, has matured her "estranged point of view." There she supports herself by the "labor of her hands" just as he did at Walden, and there she roams "as freely as the wild Indian" while criticizing human institutions with "hardly more of reverence than the Indian would feel" (p. 199). Hawthorne said of Thoreau that he had "more of the Indian in him, . . . than of any other kind of man."[22]

Hawthorne is at pains to distinguish his own attitude, if not his heroine's, from that of the author of "Civil Disobedience." He shared neither Thoreau's opposition to majority rule nor his lofty disdain for the public. In *The Scarlet Letter*, as in "Rappaccini's Daughter," he continues to hope that the artist who maintains his integrity can win popular acceptance. He shows his democratic faith in the common reader by suggesting that the community changes its attitude toward Hester and gradually learns to respect her. Hester's acts of kindness strike a responsive chord in the Puritan populace, who are more inclined to forgive her than the ruling elders. Hawthorne differentiates between the rigidity of "the wise and learned men of the community" and the leniency of the multitude (p. 162)—to put it in the terms of the preface, between the few and the many. He praises the public as a generous despot and vouches for the goodness of its heart:

> When an uninstructed multitude attempts to see with its eyes, it is exceedingly apt to be deceived. When, however, it forms its judgment, as it usually does, on the intuitions of its great

and warm heart, the conclusions thus attained are often so profound and unerring, as to possess the character of truths supernaturally revealed. [P. 127]

This recalls the similar passage in "Rappaccini's Daughter" where Beatrice urges Giovanni to trust her words rather than his eyes. In the story, Hawthorne criticized the ordinary reader for misjudging his fictions. But in the novel, as we shall see, he invites misreading by having Dimmesdale make a deceptive appeal to the multitude's uninstructed sight.

Even at its height, of course, the people's regard for Hester is slight compared to its reverence for Dimmesdale. Hawthorne, who makes much of the minister's celebrity, also takes note of the egotism that impels him to crave professional distinction. In a passage throwing light on his own motives for becoming a writer, he indicates the importance of fame in Dimmesdale's calculations:

His was a profession, at that era, in which intellectual ability displayed itself far more than in political life; for—leaving a higher motive out of the question—it offered inducements powerful enough, in the almost worshipping respect of the community, to win the most aspiring ambition into its service. Even political power—as in the case of Increase Mather—was within the grasp of a successful priest. [P. 238]

Dimmesdale fully commands this kind of popular esteem. His "Tongue of Flame," corresponding to Hawthorne's artistic gifts, enables him "to express the highest truths through the humblest medium of familiar words and images." Uniquely among the preachers of Boston he has the power "of addressing the whole human brotherhood in the heart's native language" (p. 142).

Dimmesdale has succeeded in the marketplace, but at the cost of his integrity. He has achieved his "brilliant popularity" (p. 141) not by proclaiming the truth that he is Pearl's father, since this would deeply offend his audience, but by becoming a hypocrite who wears "one face to himself, and another to the multitude" (p. 216). He has had to dissemble and equivocate to deceive his listeners into believing him a saint. Even when he speaks what is literally true, his manner of speaking converts his words into a lie. He delivers vague confessions in which he reviles himself as "the worst of sinners," knowing full well that his self-reproaches will be misinterpreted as confirmation of his sanctity. "He had spoken the very truth," Hawthorne writes of these public utterances, "and transformed it into the veriest falsehood. And yet, by the constitution of his nature, he loved the truth, and loathed the lie, as few men ever did. Therefore, above all things else, he loathed his miserable self" (pp. 143–44).

Truth is one value sacrificed in the marketplace; privacy is another. Hawthorne's fear of being violated underlies his treatment of Dimmesdale's friendship with Chillingworth. The association between the two men is an analogue for the intimate but antagonistic bond that Hawthorne feels toward the "honored reader" (p. 8), as indicated by his prefaces. The "kind and apprehensive, though not the closest friend," who he imagines listening to him talk in "The Custom-House" (p. 4), becomes in the romance proper the "kind, watchful, sympathizing, but never intrusive friend" who attends Dimmesdale as his physician (p. 130). Invited into the minister's home, just as Hawthorne invites the reader into the Old Manse, Chillingworth is the apparent friend who turns out to be an enemy. In "The Old Manse" Hawthorne tries to forbid the reader entrance into the cavern of his being, there to pore over his "treasures" or his "rubbish." Chillingworth tramples on such restraints in going "deep into his patient's bosom, delving among his principles, prying into his recollections, and probing every thing with a cautious touch, like a treasure-seeker in a dark cavern" (p. 124). Hawthorne compares him to a miner digging his way into the clergyman's heart:

> . . . after long search into the minister's dim interior, and turning over many precious materials, in the shape of high aspirations for the welfare of his race, warm love of souls, pure sentiments, natural piety, strengthened by thought and study, and illuminated by revelation,—all of which invaluable gold was perhaps no better than rubbish to the seeker,—he would turn back, discouraged, and begin his quest towards another point. He groped along as stealthily, and with as cautious a tread, and as wary an outlook, as a thief entering a chamber where a man lies only half asleep,—or, it may be, broad awake,—with purpose to steal the very treasure which this man guards as the apple of his eye. [P. 130]

Here indeed is a desecretion of the writer's private being, the "inmost Me behind its veil." In addition to the affront to the self, what seems to alarm Hawthorne about such intensive scrutiny is the possibility that the more acute among his readers will discover his complicity with Hester. In other words, just as Dimmesdale believes that the truth about him will horrify the Puritans, causing them to tear him from his pulpit, so Hawthorne fears that exposure of his unconventional side—his "Hester" side—will alienate that "great gull," the American public. Chillingworth is an example of the kind of professional critic or "eagle-eyed reader" (in Melville's phrase) who can decode the meanings lost upon the many; a single word from him would destroy Dimmesdale's standing in the community. A "man of thought," "the book-worm of great libraries" (p. 74), he has dedicated himself to ferreting out the identity of Pearl's father. "Thou mayest cover up thy secret from the prying multitude," he says to Hester when she vows to protect her lover, "But, as for me, I come to the inquest with other senses than they possess. I shall seek this man, as I have sought truth in books. . . ." Though the guilty man wears no scarlet letter on his garment, Chillingworth continues, "I shall read it on his heart" (p. 75). Elsewhere he exclaims, "Were it only for the art's sake, I must search this matter to the bottom!" (p. 138).

The search for Pearl's father is implicitly a search for the author of *The Scarlet Letter*. Hawthorne contemplates with dismay Chillingworth's speculative relish in analyzing "that child's nature, and, from its make and mould, [giving] a shrewd guess at the father" (p. 116). He feels vulnerable to such investigative activity because he identifies Pearl with his art. He describes her as a human version of his principal symbol, "the scarlet letter in another form; the scarlet letter endowed with life!" (p. 102). Hawthorne also likens Pearl to a script, "the living hieroglyphic" in which is written out the secret her parents wish to hide, and he acknowledges that "a prophet or magician skilled to read" her could deduce the father-maker from the child-text (p. 207). In fact, an analogous approach to reading literature was coming into vogue by the middle of the nineteenth century. This critical strategy, known as "symptomatic reading," construes the literary utterance as an index to the writer's history and personality. It reads backward from the artwork to the character of the artist. It is far more applicable to Hawthorne's brand of psychological romance than to conventional realism, which minimizes authorial subjectivity.[23] And Hawthorne has special reason to be wary of it as the author or "father" of thoughts unacceptable to the general public.

Although Hawthorne dreads being found out by the skillful reader, he has too much stake in acquiring fame and wealth not to brave the scrutiny of the marketplace. He cannot afford the silence of his heroine. What he keeps searching for is a resolution that will enable him to combine Dimmesdale's eminence with Hester's moral authority. *The Scarlet Letter*, then, does more than simply disclose a split in Hawthorne's thinking about his art; it tries to overcome it. In the forest scene, Hester urges Dimmesdale to flee the Puritan commonwealth; she believes that truth and intellectual freedom are possible only for the outsider. But Hawthorne, by denying the minister the alternative of flight, proposes to transcend the contradictory positions identified with his central characters. Throughout the book he has espoused his faith in the "great heart" of the people; in the final chapters, when Dimmesdale mounts the scaffold with Hester, he puts that faith to the test. He asks whether honesty can be made compatible with popularity: must the successful writer be a hypocrite? Or does he dare to speak the truth in the marketplace?

VI

The aftermath of the forest interview suggests the extent of Hawthorne's uneasiness about propounding truth to a popular audience. Hester has persuaded Dimmesdale to "exchange this false life of thine for a true one" (p. 198), and as the minister starts back to Boston, he is sorely tempted to betray his antisocial side in language. Passing an elderly deacon, he has to exercise "the most careful self-control" to "refrain from uttering certain blasphemous suggestions that rose into his mind, respecting the communion-supper" (p. 218). He longs to scandalize a pious widow with an argument against the immortality of the soul, to corrupt a young woman with a salacious whisper, and to "teach some very wicked words to a knot of Puritan children who . . . had but just begun to talk" (p. 220). The fear of exposing oneself in speech, of saying something that will undermine one's reputation, pervades this entire episode. Hawthorne yearns to be true, to admit his complicity with Hester, but he shows how dangerous and self-destructive it can be to speak one's mind freely in public.

Indeed, at this point in the narrative there seems little prospect of reconciling the two sides of Hawthorne's conflict represented by Hester and the minister, his commitment to the truth and his desire for celebrity. The lovers meet for the last time on Election Day, once again to confront "the people's eye" (p. 231). As in the novel's opening scene, Hawthorne emphasizes their sharply different circumstances, contrasting his heroine's reserve and ignominy to the preacher's eloquence and exalted stature. While Hester endures the renewed curiosity of the multitude, Dimmesdale achieves the greatest triumph of his professional career by delivering the prestigious Election Sermon. He stands "on the very proudest eminence of superiority, to which the gifts of intellect, rich lore, prevailing eloquence, and a reputation for whitest sanctity, could exalt a clergyman in New England's earliest days" (p. 249). As the procession in which he marches passes Hester, no glance of recognition is exchanged between them. The gulf separating the lovers appears too great to be bridged in the marketplace; to the wearer of the scarlet letter, the minister looks utterly "unattainable in his worldly position" (p. 239).

The Election Sermon itself explores one possible way out of this impasse: communicating truth in public not by openly confessing but by incorporating two separate layers of meaning into a single discourse. On the surface, Dimmesdale's sermon is calculated to enhance his prestige with the Puritans. Its subject, according to Hawthorne, is the providential mission of New England. The minister has assured his hearers of "a high and glorious destiny for the newly gathered people of the Lord" (p. 249), and the colonists show their delight in his performance by a tremendous shout of acclamation. But the stated message of the sermon is at odds with the implied meaning of its undertone, which is understood only by Hester. A tremor in the minister's voice conveys "the complaint of a human heart, sorrow-laden, perchance guilty, telling its secret, whether of guilt or sorrow, to the great heart of mankind; beseeching its sympathy or forgiveness,—at every moment,—in each accent,—and never in vain!" (pp. 243–44). Although the colonists hear the undertone, they misinterpret it as "the natural regret of one soon to pass away" (p. 249). The two layers of meaning, public celebration and private sinfulness, national election and "blackness," correspond to Hawthorne's conflicting wishes to be popular and to tell the truth, but only one meaning is accessible to the many. The minister flatters the sensibilities of the multitude while opening his heart to a select audience of the initiate. The Dimmesdale of the Election Sermon comes closer to Melville's notion of the artist as confidence man than to Hawthorne's ideal of integrity in the marketplace.

The sermon is plainly unacceptable as a solution to Hawthorne's predicament; its approach to the public is elitist rather than democratic. It violates Hawthorne's conviction that "the great heart of mankind" is an infallible court of appeal. Even its admission of guilt is equivocal because it occurs in a medium other than language. Dimmesdale's undertone is inarticulate, a shriek or cry that Hawthorne compares to music and the wind. As Hester listens to it, she stands at too great a distance from the meetinghouse to comprehend the sermon. Hawthorne says that the discourse had "a meaning for her, entirely apart from its indistinguishable words" (p. 243).

Hawthorne's democratic principles require a genuine confession in speech, one that the mass public can understand. Although he fears the consequences of self-disclosure almost as much as the minister, he has no choice but to return Dimmesdale to the scaffold for a final "revelation of the scarlet letter." This time the Puritan divine seems resolved "to speak out the whole" of his secret (p. 255). He turns aside Chillingworth's plea when the old man tries to dissuade him from confessing: "Do not blacken your fame, and perish in dishonor! . . . Would you bring infamy on your sacred profession?" (p. 252). Hawthorne expresses confidence that the many will accept and forgive the minister's unveiling of his "inmost Me." The people's heart, he writes, "was thoroughly appalled, yet overflowing with tearful sympathy, as knowing that some deep life-matter—which, if full of sin, was full of anguish and repentance likewise—was now to be laid open to them" (p. 254).

What Dimmesdale actually says, however, falls considerably short of his avowed objective of openness in the marketplace. At the beginning of his confession, he addresses the Puritans in the first person. "Behold me here," he cries, "the one sinner of the world! . . . I stand upon the spot where, seven years since, I should have stood; here, with this woman" (p. 254). Then a change occurs: Dimmesdale abruptly begins to refer to himself in the third person. "It was on him!" he continues.

> "God's eye beheld it! The angels were for ever pointing at it! The Devil knew it well, and fretted it continually with the touch of his burning finger! But he hid it cunningly from men, and walked among you with the mien of a spirit, mournful, because so pure in a sinful world!—and sad, because he missed his heavenly kindred! Now, at the death-hour, he stands up before you! He bids you look again at Hester's scarlet letter! He tells you, that, with all its mysterious horror, it is but the shadow of what he bears on his own breast, and that even that, his own red stigma, is no more than the type of what has seared his inmost heart! Stand any here that question God's judgment on a sinner? Behold! Behold a dreadful witness of it." [P. 255]

The shift from "I" to "he" in Dimmesdale's speech is analogous to the shift in *The Scarlet Letter* from the "I" of "The Custom-House" to the "he" of "The Scarlet Letter." It is no longer clear whom the clergyman is talking about; as with the text itself, there has been a retreat from the promise of intimate revelation to distancing and impersonality.

Hawthorne's faith in the generosity of the many shatters against his fear of alienating the common reader. He has Dimmesdale address a last appeal to the people's heart, not by using language, but by acting out a gesture with his body. The minister shows rather than speaks the secret of his relation with Hester. Previously Hawthorne said that the multitude is "exceedingly apt to be deceived" when it "attempts to see with its eyes." At the climax of his ambiguous confession, Dimmesdale tears away his clerical band and exposes his breast to "the gaze of the horror-stricken multitude" (p. 255). The colonists express their "awe and wonder" by a collective murmur "that rolled . . . heavily after the departed spirit," but it is impossible to know what they are responding to since they differ among themselves about what they have witnessed (p. 257). Some deny having seen anything at all on the minister's breast, others disagree in their interpretations of the stigma's significance. Little wonder that Chillingworth is heard to mutter, "Hadst thou sought the whole earth over, there was no one place so secret . . . save on this very scaffold!" (p. 253). Dimmesdale's "revelation of the scarlet letter" has turned out to be fully as evasive as the autobiographical disclosures with which Hawthorne prefaces his fictions, disclosures, as he keeps protesting, which "hide the man, instead of displaying him." [24]

Hawthorne, in short, is unable to overcome his doubts about the wisdom of telling the truth to a mass audience. Like Dimmesdale, he rejects clarity in favor of obfuscation as a mode of treating with the public, a strategy of exchange. At the end of *The Scarlet Letter*, he links his readers to the spectators in the Boston marketplace and leaves them as much in the dark as the most befuddled Puritan. He imitates the minister's avoidance of direct speech by refusing to describe what has happened on the scaffold. When Dimmesdale unbosoms, he says only, "it were irreverent to describe that revelation" (p. 255); of the various reactions to the scene, he merely comments, "The reader may choose among these theories" (p. 259). Even the moral he assigns to the tale, in his capacity as its "editor," is a masterpiece of equivocation. "Be true! Be true!" he exclaims, and then he adds ambiguously, "Show freely to the world, if not your worst, yet some trait whereby the worst may be inferred!" (p. 260).

The Scarlet Letter closes on a note of ambiguity, but ambiguity is not the same as lying. Hawthorne began his narrative with two opposed images of the artist, the silent but moral outsider and the popular success who is a hypocrite. He ends it by modifying the first possibility and rejecting the second, formulating two new versions of the nineteenth-century man of letters, types of the modern writer created by the pressures of commercialization. Hester continues to represent the Thoreau-like possibility of truthfulness combined with indifference to worldly goods. Hawthorne relates that his feminine protagonist, having returned to New England after many years abroad, "had no selfish ends, nor lived in any measure for her own profit" (p. 263). She differs in one important respect from the Hester who refused to speak in the novel's opening moments. The youthful Hester kept her own counsel about the social injustices suffered by women. The Hester of the "Conclusion" freely speaks her thoughts about the future reformation of society, which she believes will be inspired by "a new truth" about relations between the sexes (p. 263). She becomes a dissenting intellectual on the margins, criticizing the status quo to the few who are similarly disaffected. Although she expresses herself openly in language now, she holds forth, not in the marketplace, but at her cottage on the periphery of the settlement.

Dimmesdale, if not quite unguarded in the marketplace, nevertheless ceases his false life of pandering to the popular taste. He refuses to continue as a conscious hypocrite who values public adulation above all else. After the minister utters his last words to the multitude from behind a mask of impersonality, he collapses and dies. To tell a version of the truth, however ambiguous, he effaces his individual identity, figuratively by changing voice to "he," literally by dying. The final scene on the scaffold anticipates the modernist strategy whereby the author absents himself from his text in order to speak—precisely the strategy Melville attributed to Hawthorne in the "Mosses" essay. The final scaffold scene also looks backward to the introductory sketch, which Hawthorne brings to a conclusion by announcing his figurative death. He describes his expulsion from office as a political beheading and proposes that the ensuing narrative be regarded as the "*Posthumous Papers of a Decapitated Surveyor.*" Claiming to write "from beyond the grave," he enters the marketplace as a symbolic dead man to tell his own version of the truth, the revealing but impersonal narrative of "The Scarlet Letter" (pp. 43–

44). His novel, like the later fictions of Melville, comes into being through the suppression of the writer's person. For Hawthorne, the "death of the author"[25] is a direct consequence of the necessity to speak in the public marketplace rather than being supported by an individual patron or a circle of aristocratic intimates. The writer "dies" because he has to find some way to survive in what has become purely a relation of exchange.

5

The Artist and the Marketplace in

The House of the Seven Gables

I

The fairy-tale ending of *The House of the Seven Gables* has not satisfied the novel's modern readers, most of whom have agreed with F. O. Matthiessen that "the reconciliation [of Maule and Pyncheon] is somewhat too lightly made" and that in bestowing the Judge's ill-gotten wealth upon the surviving characters, Hawthorne evidently overlooked his own warnings about the evils of inheritance.[1] William Charvat has suggested that the ending's weakness may stem less from authorial oversight than from the requirements of the marketplace. While noting that Hawthorne himself seems to have shared the popular preference for fiction combining "sunshine and shadow," Charvat points out that he was also alert to "the professional or commercial aspects of his project." Despite the moderate success of *The Scarlet Letter*, he was still hard pressed financially and knew only too well that his reputation for "blackness" (as Melville termed it) was an obstacle to acceptance by the wider public. "We cannot ignore the possibility," adds Charvat, "that Hawthorne, in concluding his book as he did, was yielding to the world's wish that in stories everything should turn out well."[2]

In fact, it seems considerably more than a possibility. The text itself reveals a Hawthorne deeply concerned with his relation to the public and with his priorities as a writer who both craved fame and money

This chapter originally appeared in a slightly different form under the same title in *ELH* 48 (1981): 172–89. Reprinted by permission of The Johns Hopkins University Press.

and aspired—again in Melville's words—to be a master of "the great Art of Telling the Truth." Melville's famous review of *Mosses from an Old Manse* appeared just as Hawthorne began work on *The House of the Seven Gables*. "In this world of lies," Melville had argued, profound authors had no choice but to become deceivers, to hoodwink the general reader by concealing their meanings.[3] But Hawthorne could not share Melville's apparent equanimity about adopting his strategy. He reacted with pain and dismay when he found himself obliged to employ it in his work-in-progress, and he was unable to suppress his misgivings that in bowing to the marketplace he was compromising his artistic independence and integrity.

II

Hawthorne states in the preface to *The House of the Seven Gables* that the romantic character of his tale consists in its being "a Legend, prolonging itself, from an epoch now gray in the distance, down into our own broad daylight, and bringing along with it some of its legendary mist" (p. 2). He proceeds in the opening chapter to speak of hereditary curses and ghostly powers, but his conception of the legendary is not confined to the paraphernalia of gothic romance.[4] He is also referring to that body of knowledge and speculation which is excluded from the officially sanctioned view of things. The legendary encompasses the "rumors," "traditions," and "fables" that necessarily remain clandestine and underground because they express truths too controversial for public utterance. In discussing Colonel Pyncheon's designs on the Maule homestead, Hawthorne observes, "No written record of this dispute is known to be in existence. Our acquaintance with the whole subject is derived chiefly from tradition" (p. 7). Tradition is also his sole authority for intimating a connection between the executed wizard's curse—"God will give him blood to drink"—and the mysterious manner of the Colonel's death. The Colonel's laudatory funeral sermon, "which was printed and is still extant," contains no hint of guilt and retribution. "Tradition—which sometimes brings down truth that history has let slip, but is oftener the wild babble of the time, such as was formerly spoken at the fireside, and now congeals in newspapers—tradition is responsible for all contrary averments" (p. 17). The imputation of troubled consciences to the Colonel's descendants is similarly laid to the town's "traditionary gossips" and to "impressions too vaguely founded to be put on paper" (p. 20).

Despite this last remark, the distinction being made here is not primarily between speech and writing. Hawthorne contrasts spoken words and written ones only insofar as they lend support to the more fundamental distinction between private and public discourse. Criticism of the Pyncheons is more likely to be expressed orally than on paper because the "written record," historical or otherwise, is addressed to the world and dare not impeach the characters of eminent men whom all the world agrees in honoring. The awareness of a potentially unsympathetic audience can be inhibiting to the artist and work against truthfulness in any medium of expression.

This notion is implicit in Hawthorne's discussion of Judge Pyncheon. After noting that no one—neither inscriber of tombstones, nor public speaker, nor writer of history—would venture a word of censure against the Judge, he continues:

> But besides these cold, formal, and empty words of the chisel that inscribes, the voice that speaks, and the pen that writes for the public eye and for distant time—and which inevitably lose much of their truth and freedom by the fatal consciousness of so doing—there were traditions about the ancestor, and private diurnal gossip about the Judge, remarkably accordant in their testimony. It is often instructive to take the woman's, the private and domestic view, of a public man; nor can anything be more curious than the vast discrepancy between portraits intended for engraving, and the pencil-sketches that pass from hand to hand, behind the original's back. [P. 122]

The reference in this passage to loss of truth and freedom has obvious relevance for an author who claims in his preface "a certain latitude" as a writer of romance and who takes as his subject "the truth of the human heart" (p. 1). By extending his observations to the difference between engravings and pencil sketches, moreover, Hawthorne suggests that a major reason for circumspection in addressing the public is the fear of offending potential customers. The inference that the wisdom associated with the legendary is not only guarded and private but unsalable emerges clearly from his description of the Colonel's portrait hanging in the house of the seven gables. With the passage of time, the portrait's superficial coloring has faded and the inward traits of its subject have grown more prominent and striking. Such an effect, Hawthorne notes, is not uncommon in antique paintings: "They acquire a look which an artist (if he have anything like the complaisancy of artists, now-a-days) would never dream of presenting to a patron as his own characteristic expression, but which, nevertheless, we at once recognize as reflecting the unlovely truth of a human soul" (p. 59). In other words, the artist who is determined to express the truth openly in the present will find it impossible to sell his creations.

Perhaps the key word in Hawthorne's description of the contemporary artist is "complaisancy." Whether the prospective buyer is an individual patron or the general public, the artist has to appear accommodating if he wishes to succeed in the marketplace. He cannot afford to be honest because his truth-telling may alienate his audience and deprive him of his livelihood. Although Hawthorne is speaking here of the portrait painter in particular, his analysis applies to anyone involved in the process of exchange. In *The House of the Seven Gables* he comments most directly on the exchange process and the relation of buyer and seller in the chapters devoted to Hepzibah's opening of her cent-shop.

Finding herself practically destitute after a lifetime of patrician indolence, Hepzibah has decided to try her hand at business when the narrative proper opens in contemporary Salem. Although she herself cares little for material comforts, she expects the imminent return of her brother Clifford from jail and refuses to apply for financial assistance to their cousin the Judge, the man she holds responsible for Clifford's long imprisonment. With no other recourse but to support Clifford by her own exertions, she has mustered her courage to reopen the little shop built into the house by a penurious ancestor and long regarded as an embarrassment by the family. Hawthorne, in his capacity as "a disembodied listener" (p. 30), follows her protracted preparations for the first day behind the counter with a mixture of sympathy and satire. She is introduced sighing at her toilet as she struggles to overcome her reluctance about facing the world. At least twice she pauses before her toilet glass in a pathetic attempt to make herself look attractive. Stepping at last into the passageway, she slowly makes her way through the house to the shop's entrance and with a sudden effort thrusts herself across the threshold. Her hesitation returns inside the shop and she nervously sets about rearranging the goods in the window. Still she hangs back from "the public eye" (p. 39), as if, writes Hawthorne, she expected to come before the community "like a disembodied divinity, or enchantress, holding forth her bargains to the reverential and awe-striken purchaser, in an invisible hand" (p. 40). Unlike Hawthorne himself, however, she is not permitted the luxury of invisibility: "She was well aware that she must ultimately come forward and stand revealed in her proper individuality; but, like other sensitive persons, she could not bear to be observed in the gradual process, and chose rather to flash forth on the world's astonished gaze, at once" (p. 40).

Hepzibah strikingly recalls Hester Prynne standing in the marketplace with her badge of shame and suffering "under the heavy weight of a thousand unrelenting eyes."[5] As Hepzibah takes her place behind the counter, she too is tortured "with a sense of overwhelming shame, that strange and unloving eyes should have the privilege of gazing" at her (p. 46). In recounting her tribulations, Hawthorne dwells on the importance of being seen in trade and making a favorable impression. Hepzibah herself feels continued uneasiness over the appearance of the window: "It seemed as if the whole fortune or failure of her shop might depend on the display of a different set of articles, or substituting a fairer apple for one which appeared to be specked" (pp. 46–47). Repeatedly Hawthorne calls attention to the handicap of her scowl, which results from nearsightedness but has unfortunately given her the reputation of being ill tempered. When that shrewd Yankee Dixey passes by her shop, he loudly predicts that Hepzibah's frown will be her financial undoing. "Make it go!" he exclaims. "Not a bit of it! Why her face—I've seen it . . . her face is enough to frighten Old Nick himself, if he had ever so great a mind to trade with her" (p. 47). Overhearing these words, Hepzibah has a painful vision that seems to underscore the futility of her venture. On one side of the street stands her antiquated shop, over which she presides with an offending scowl, and on the other rises a magnificent bazaar, "with a multitude of perfumed and glossy salesmen, smirking, smiling, bowing, and measuring out the goods!" (p. 49). Even the simple-minded Uncle Venner, who offers Hepzibah encouragement along with maxims cribbed from Poor Richard, advocates a beaming countenance as "all-important" to success in business: "Put on a bright face for your customers, and smile pleasantly as you hand them what they ask for! A stale article, if you dip it in a good, warm, sunny smile, will go off better than a fresh one that you've scowled upon!" (p. 66).

As such passages suggest, Hawthorne is using Hepzibah to explore his own ambivalence about courting the public in order to make money. Although she herself is not an artist figure, she resembles her creator both in her history of isolation and her need to earn a living. One thinks immediately of Hawthorne's seclusion for thirteen years after graduating from Bowdoin and his self-designation as "the obscurest man of letters in America."[6] It is no wonder that he gives Hepzibah a Puritan progenitor who was involved in the witchcraft trials like his own ancestor John Hathorne, and who appears in his portrait much as William Hathorne is described in "The Custom-House," clutching a Bible and a sword. As an author who always insisted upon preserving his privacy, Hawthorne would not have found it difficult to appreciate Hepzibah's misgivings about encountering "the public gaze" (p. 35). He would have understood her resentment at the familiar tone adopted by her customers, who "evidently considered themselves not merely her equals but her patrons and superiors" (p. 54). Indeed, he draws an implicit parallel between his writing and the commodities she hopes to sell. Her stock consists primarily of items of food like applies, Indian meal, and gingerbread men, and in the preface he speaks of his book as an object to be eaten, calling it a "dish offered to the Public" (p. 1). And he seems almost as hesitant about getting his narrative under way as she does about opening her business. Just as she pauses apprehensively on the threshold of her shop, so "we are loitering faint-heartedly," says Hawthorne, "on the threshold of our story" (p. 34).

Despite his sympathy for her discomfort, Hawthorne is far from identifying with Hepzibah uncritically. A part of him yearned "to open an intercourse with the world" and was capable of plotting with his publisher to outwit the general reader.[7] This part finds her more comical than tragic and strongly disapproves of her reluctance to seek her own fortune. Although Hawthorne himself had difficulty supporting his family by his writing, and lobbied actively for government appointments, in print he commends the marketplace for fostering self-reliance and expresses detached amusement at Hepzibah's dreams of being rescued from trade by a sudden bequest. Too much of a democrat to endorse her aristocratic pretensions, he agrees with Holgrave that she will discover satisfaction in contributing her mite "to the united struggle of mankind" (p. 45). Her first sale does in fact bring her an unexpected sense of accomplishment and dispels many of her fears about commerce with the world. But she lacks both the skill and the temperament to prosper as a saleswoman, and at the end of the day she has as little to show for "all her painful traffic" (p. 67) as Hawthorne did after his long apprentieship as a writer of tales and sketches.

It is through Phoebe rather than Hepzibah herself that Hawthorne expresses his conviction—or more precisely his hope—that it is possible to be engaged in market relations without suffering a sense of violation. Phoebe, who has "had a table at a fancy-fair, and made better sales than anybody," is able to drive a shrewd bargain relying only on her "native truth and sagacity" (pp. 78–79). Her practical mind abounds with schemes "whereby the influx of trade might be increased, and rendered profitable, without a hazardous outlay of capital" (p. 79). Her smile is unconscious of itself, and therefore honest and spontaneous; for her it is a simple matter, in Uncle Venner's phrase, to "put on a bright face for [her] customers." As Hawthorne often states, she has a naturally sunny disposition, and her presence is like "a gleam of sunshine" in the gloomy old house (p. 80). Hepzibah is quick to acknowledge her superiority as a shopkeeper, and the public shows its agreement by flocking to the store during the hours when she takes her turn behind the counter.

No doubt Hawthorne wishes for comparable good fortune in his dealings with the public. But he seems to have suspected that his own sunny smile was not nearly so ready as Phoebe's. And he was aware of the possibilities for deception in exchange relations, being based as they are so largely on appearance. There is one character in particular in *The House of the Seven Gables* who thoroughly appreciates the marketability of a genial countenance, and who incurs the censure that Hawthorne feels toward his own worldly ambition.[8] Although his natural expression is anything but cheerful, Judge Jaffrey Pyncheon has worked up an extraordinary smile for public consumption. The passages describing his sham joviality are remarkable in Hawthorne's writing for their unrelieved hostility and exaggerated irony. In chapter 7, "The Pyncheon of To-day," where he first tries to gain an interview with Clifford, he puts on an especially dazzling face to win the confidence of Hepzibah and Phoebe. As he enters the house, "his smile grew as intense as if he had set his heart on counteracting the whole gloom of the atmosphere . . . by the unassisted light of his countenance" (p. 117). Advancing to greet Hepzibah, he wears a smile "so broad and sultry, that had it been only half as warm as it looked, a trellis of grapes might at once have turned purple under its summer-like exposure" (p. 127). Of course the Judge's sunshiny exterior only masks his darker purposes, and his smile changes to a frown like a thundercloud when his wishes are opposed. But Jaffrey is too practiced a hypocrite to allow himself to be caught off guard for very long. Hawthorne devotes an entire paragraph to the ingratiating manner with which he covers his departure:

With a bow to Hepzibah, and a degree of paternal benevolence in his parting nod to Phoebe, the Judge left the shop,
and went smiling along the street. As is customary with the
rich, when they aim at the honors of a republic, he apologized,
as it were, to the people, for his wealth, prosperity, and ele-
vated station, by a free and hearty manner towards those who
knew him; putting off the more of his dignity, in due proportion with the humbleness of the man whom he saluted; and
thereby proving a haughty consciousness of his advantages, as
irrefragably as if he had marched forth, preceded by a troop of
lackeys to clear the way. On this particular forenoon, so excessive was the warmth of Judge Pyncheon's kindly aspect, that
(such, at least, was the rumor about town) an extra passage of
water-carts was found essential, in order to lay the dust occa-
sioned by so much extra sunshine! [Pp. 130–31]

The Judge clearly has much in common with the oily, grinning salesmen of Hepzibah's vision. He also bears a marked resemblance to the
Italian organ-grinder's monkey, who performs "a bow and scrape"
(p. 164) while holding out his palm to receive the public's money.

The Judge has been well rewarded for his assiduous cultivation of
the public. Whereas Hepzibah's scowl threatens to ruin her, his smile
has brought him every imaginable success. He is very rich, enjoys the
reputation of a model citizen, and has been showered with public
honors, including election to Congress. "Beyond all question," states
Hawthorne, he "was a man of eminent respectability. The church acknowledged it; the state acknowledged it. It was denied by nobody"
(p. 228). This assessment occurs in chapter 15, "The Scowl and Smile,"
where Hawthorne also hints of perceptions more discerning than the
world's. In an elaborate metaphor, he compares Jaffrey's public personality to a glittering and sunbathed palace, "which, in the view of
other people, and ultimately in his own view, is no other than the
man's character, or the man himself" (p. 229). But in some concealed
nook of this splendid edifice, inaccessible to public view,

may lie a corpse, half-decayed, and still decaying, and diffusing
its death-scent through the palace! The inhabitant will not be
conscious of it, for it has long been his daily breath! Neither
will the visitors, for they smell only the rich odors which the
master sedulously scatters through the palace. . . . Now and
then, perchance, comes in a seer, before whose sadly gifted eye
the whole structure melts into thin air, leaving only the hidden

nook, the bolted closet, with the cobwebs festooned over its forgotten door, or the deadly hole under the pavement, and the decaying corpse within. Here, then, we are to seek the true emblem of the man's character, and of the deed which gives whatever reality it possesses to his life. And, beneath the show of a marble palace, that pool of stagnant water, foul with many impurities, and, perhaps, tinged with blood,—that secret abomination, above which, possibly, he may say his prayers, without remembering it,—is this man's miserable soul! [P. 230]

In this passage Hawthorne implicitly repudiates any connection between his own art and Jaffrey's manipulation of appearances. Jaffrey is an "artist" of the public, but Hawthorne's seer is an artist of the private, of the legendary. His unflattering vision of the human soul is no more marketable than the antique portrait of the Colonel; he could never hope to present it either to the public or to the builder of the palace. Insofar as Hawthorne seeks to portray "the truth of the human heart," he himself is such an artist.

The figure in *The House of the Seven Gables* who most closely approximates this kind of artist is Holgrave, the daguerreotypist and descendant of the wizard. From the moment of their dispossession the Maules have been associated with ghostly powers, poverty, and secrecy. They are said to have outwardly cherished "no malice against individuals or the public, for the wrong which had been done them." Any grievances they may have felt were transmitted "at their own fireside" and "never acted upon, nor openly expressed" (p. 25). Down through the generations they have been marked off from other men by their "character of reserve" and by a self-imposed isolation which has kept them from prospering (p. 26). Holgrave, who appears in the text under the veil of an assumed name, has carried the family traditions into the present. Suspected of practicing the Black Art, he holds views subversive of established authority and generally remains aloof from the society of others. As he tells Phoebe, his impulse is not to bare his heart in public but "to look on, to analyze, to explain matters to myself" (p. 216). Even more than Hepzibah, he suggests the side of Hawthorne that dominates the prefaces—the Hawthorne who insists on veiling his countenance from the reader's gaze and claims that his seeming intimacies "hide the man, instead of displaying him."[9] He further resembles his creator, who spent a year at Brook Farm, in his association with reformers and "community-men" (p. 84). And he writes stories which he supposedly contributes to periodicals where Hawthorne's own tales have appeared, such as *Graham's Magazine* and Godey's *Magazine and Lady's Book.*

Holgrave, in other words, is like Hawthorne before he wrote *The Scarlet Letter* and became known to the wider public. He obviously has earned little money from his periodical writing, and when Phoebe professes ignorance of his efforts, he exclaims much as the younger Hawthorne might have, "Well; such is literary fame!" (p. 186). The sample of his work reprinted in *The House of the Seven Gables*, "Alice Pyncheon," helps to explain his lack of success with the average reader. Like the larger text of which it forms a part, it tells a story of conflict between the Maules and Pyncheons, but it goes beyond Hawthorne's own narrative in its incautious use of the half-spoken and the legendary. The tale has Matthew Maule openly assert both his right to the house and his power over Alice, thus giving centrality to the very themes of class resentment and psychic mastery that Hawthorne tends to treat with circumspection. In writing it, as Holgrave says, he has essentially followed "wild, chimney-corner legend" (p. 197), and in general he shows neither aptitude nor inclination for an art that will be popular. His daguerreotypes, to borrow the distinction made by Hawthorne, are more like pencil sketches that have to be passed behind the subject's back than portraits suitable for engraving. Holgrave, who realizes this himself, explains to Phoebe that his photographic images bring out "the secret character with a truth that no painter would ever venture upon, even could he detect it. There is at least no flattery in my humble line of art" (p. 91). He then shows her a daguerreotype miniature of the Judge that in the manner of the Colonel's portrait reveals "the unlovely truth of a human soul." Remarkably enough, according to Holgrave, "the original wears, to the world's eye . . . an exceedingly pleasant countenance, indicative of benevolence, openness of heart, sunny good humor, and other praiseworthy qualities of that cast." The face in the daguerreotype, however, is "sly, subtle, hard, imperious, and, withal, cold as ice." The picture's very truthfulness, of course, will make it impossible to sell; as Holgrave observes, "It is so much the more unfortunate, as [the original] is a public character of some eminence, and the likeness was intended to be engraved" (p. 92).

While Hawthorne clearly put much of himself into the daguerreotypist, it would be a mistake to exaggerate their similarities. Rather, as the preface to *The Snow-Image* suggests, one must "look through the whole range of his fictitious characters, good and evil, in order to detect any of his essential traits."[10] The author of *The House of the*

Seven Gables had too much need of money to identify completely with Holgrave's indifference to popularity. With only his writing to support himself and his family, he could not afford to despise the commercial advantage of a pleasing exterior. And while he might sympathize with Hepzibah, it is her cousin the Judge whom "the world's laudatory voice" has acclaimed and enriched (p. 229). The conflict between Maule and Pyncheon, Holgrave and Jaffrey, is accordingly a conflict in Hawthorne's own mind. It reflects the division in his view of the artist as "a man of society" who appeals to the general reader [11] and as a private teller of truth whose revelations are unsalable. Hawthorne's second novel thus poses many of the same questions as his first one, questions about the relation between integrity and popularity. To gain acceptance with the public, is it necessary to become a hypocrite like the Judge? Is it possible to depict the truth of the heart like Holgrave without sacrificing commercial success? Who is the rightful owner of the house of the seven gables? Of *The House of the Seven Gables*? What kind of artist is Hawthorne finally to be?

III

Hawthorne attempts to resolve this dilemma by reconciling Maule and Pyncheon and writing a book of truth that will attract a popular audience. He proposes to bring the legendary mist into "our own broad daylight" and to prove that Holgrave's insights are compatible with Phoebe's smile. Along with many of his readers, he had been troubled by the lack of "cheering light" in *The Scarlet Letter* and attributed its popularity primarily to the introductory sketch. He had written in "The Custom-House" that the story of Hester and the minister "wears, to my eye, a stern and sombre aspect; too much ungladdened by genial sunshine; too little relieved by the tender and familiar influences which soften almost every scene of nature and real life, and, undoubtedly, should soften every picture of them." [12] Reviewers, including Hawthorne's favorite critic, E. P. Whipple, agreed. The book was too uniformly gloomy to please the general public. [13] In his second novel, Hawthorne was determined to remedy this commercial failing by alleviating his customary blackness with a liberal use of "genial sunshine."

The finished work does in fact avoid the relentlessly tragic tone of *The Scarlet Letter*. Although the narrative voice sometimes sounds as radical as Holgrave, many passages reveal a penchant for sentiment and fancy. Like the daguerreotypist, Hawthorne questions the integrity of great men and the political system that promotes them. In speaking of Jaffrey's gubernatorial ambitions, for example, he refers to the backroom politicians who "steal from the people, without its knowledge, the power of choosing its own rulers . . . . This little knot of subtle schemers will control the convention, and, through it, dictate to the party" (p. 274). But these cynical reflections tend to alternate with heart-warming affirmations worthy of Phoebe. The Hawthorne who writes of the bees sent by God "to gladden our poor Clifford" (p. 148), or who gushes over his young heroine's domesticity, seems less an artist of the legendary than a pen-and-ink man addressing "the intellect and sympathies of the multitude."[14] And of course the clearest indication of Hawthorne's wish to effect a compromise between Maule and Pyncheon is the romance of Holgrave and Phoebe. Both characters give up some of their family traits and move toward a common ground. Admitting that his "legend" will never do for a popular audience, the daguerreotypist refrains from exercising the psychic power of the Maules and discovers a new respect for institutions. Phoebe, who has shed some of her sunshine as a result of living in the house, becomes "more womanly, and deep-eyed, in token of a heart that had begun to suspect its depths" (p. 297). Hawthorne's art comes to rest at the dead center of their marriage; in contrast to "Alice Pyncheon," which ends unhappily, the novel itself finds a way to combine salability with knowledge of the heart.

Or does it? If, as Hawthorne insisted, the book was "more proper and natural" for him to write than *The Scarlet Letter*,[15] why did he experience difficulty in completing it? According to Charvat, he probably began work in the late summer of 1850, made steady progress, and hoped to finish by November. His publishers, Ticknor, Reed, and Fields, began to advertise "A new Romance by the author of 'The Scarlet Letter'" in the October *Literary World*, and looked forward to having the completed manuscript in their hands by December 1. But Hawthorne slowed down unexpectedly after his rapid start and confessed to James T. Fields on November 29 that the conclusion was giving him particular problems: "It darkens damnably towards the close, but I shall try hard to pour some setting sunshine over it." The effort proved more troublesome and disturbing than Hawthorne anticipated, as is evident from a letter dated ten days later: "My desire and prayer is, to get through with the business already in hand . . . . I have been in a Slough of Despond, for some days past—having written so fiercely that I came to a stand still.

There are points where a writer gets bewildered, and cannot form any judgment of what he has done, nor tell what to do next." As late as January 12, only two weeks before the completion date given in the preface, he wrote to Fields that he was still "hammering away a little on the roof, and doing up a few odd jobs that were left incomplete." The tinkering continued, Charvat believes, until Hawthorne sent the book to the printers.[16]

There is no way of knowing precisely what changes Hawthorne made to lighten the novel's mood and bring it to "a prosperous close."[17] But hints scattered throughout the final pages support the notion that he was unhappy with his happy ending. At one point he writes that the house continued to diffuse a gloom "which no brightness of the sunshine could dispel" (p. 296); and elsewhere he compares his story to "an owl, bewildered in the daylight" (p. 268). The owl suggests Hepzibah, squinting and frowning in the glare of the public gaze, and Hawthorne used the same word, "bewildered," when he complained of his difficulties with the ending. The comic resolution demanded by his readers, he clearly felt, was violating the logic of his tale and covering up its scowl with an inappropriate smile.

This supposition is also suggested by Hawthorne's treatment of Holgrave in the book's concluding chapters. In chapter 20, "The Flower of Eden," the daguerreotypist declares his love for Phoebe and renounces his radicalism. Henceforth he will confine himself "within ancient limits" and even "build a house for another generation" (p. 307). His sudden reversal of character has left most readers unconvinced. But in reality Holgrave shows great reluctance, as Hawthorne notes, "to betake himself within the precincts of common life" (p. 305). He is particularly loath to publicize "the awful secret" (p. 305) of the Judge's death, and the reasons he gives for his hesitation are not very consistent. Supposedly he fears that Clifford's flight will be construed as an admission of guilt, yet he also says that Jaffrey's death, being "attended by none of those suspicious circumstances" which surrounded the uncle's death, will clear Clifford of the earlier crime (p. 304). Phoebe is at a loss to comprehend his indecision. While he keeps putting off the moment of disclosure, she pleads with him not "to hide this thing. . . . It is dreadful to keep it so closely in our hearts. Clifford is innocent. God will make it manifest! Let us throw open the doors, and call all the neighborhood to see the truth!" (p. 305). The "truth" in question is the knowledge of the heart, and herein lies the deeper reason for Holgrave's unwillingness to make it known. Jaffrey's body in the house of the seven gables recalls the stately palace with its hidden secret, and the daguerreotypist, who takes a picture of the scene, corresponds to the seer whose "sadly gifted eye" detects the corpse within, "the true emblem" of the man's soul. But this truth, which is also the truth of Hawthorne's art, has been characterized throughout the book as private and unsalable; in revealing it to the public, Holgrave is "inevitably" corrupted "by the fatal consciousness of so doing." His action betrays his calling as an artist of the legendary and is precisely analogous to Hawthorne's contrivance of a happy ending at the expense of narrative consistency. Though the results in both cases may be "Pretty good business," as Dixey puts it (p. 319), Holgrave's reluctance to capitulate is also his creator's.

Hawthorne, to be sure, might have been masking his deeper intentions and inviting an ironic reading that emphasizes the discrepancy between appearance and reality.[18] Melville, it will be remembered, recommended this strategy for the author "too deserving of popularity to be popular,"[19] and in the final chapters Hawthorne tries to make a virtue of necessity by implying that his story's surface is at odds with its inner meaning. When the summer storm subsides the morning after the Judge's death, he points out that the sunshine creates a false impression of the house. "So little faith is due to external appearance, that there was really an inviting aspect over the venerable edifice, conveying an idea that its history must be a decorous and happy one" (p. 285). Several pages later, when the organ-grinder stops to play on Pyncheon street, he continues: "to us, who know the inner heart of the seven gables, as well as its exterior face, there is a ghastly effect in this representation of light popular tunes at its doorstep" (p. 294).

Hawthorne's insistence on the disjunction between the house's outward face and its interior is echoed by Holgrave in the book's concluding chapter. As the triumphant party of survivors prepares to take possession of the Judge's country mansion, the daguerreotypist wonders why the dead man did not see fit to embody "so excellent a piece of domestic architecture in stone, rather than in wood. Then, every generation of the family might have altered the interior, to suit its own taste and convenience; while the exterior, through the lapse of years, might have been adding venerableness to its original beauty, thus giving that impression of permanence, which I consider essential to the happiness of any one moment" (pp. 314–15). In one sense this statement represents a compromise between reform and conservatism.[20] Equally important, it advocates a policy of deception with regard to houses, and as such it is also a statement about Hawthorne's art. In the preface he likened the writing of his tale to "building a house, of materials long in use for constructing castles in the air" (p. 3), and of course the title of his novel is *The House of the Seven Gables*.

Hawthorne, then, appears to have agreed with Melville's view of the artist as a con man; certainly he *wanted* to accept it in order to justify his surrender to the marketplace. But the narrative itself repudiates this strategy as morally reprehensible, and Hawthorne stands condemned for employing it by the value system of his own art. Though appearances may be unreliable in the novel, only one character makes a practice of deliberate deception. Hepzibah's heart is often said to smile while her face is frowning, but she cannot help herself. Hawthorne does the opposite: he smiles while his heart is frowning. In contrast to Phoebe's "natural sunshine" (p. 297), the "warm, sunny smile" he presents to the reader is contrived and artificial. He had to try hard, as he admitted to Fields, to pour sunshine over the tale's darkening close, and in doing so he follows the example of Judge Pyncheon manufacturing a sunny exterior to win the favor of the public. Passages that denounce the villain for hypocrisy became ironically self-accusing when considered in relation to the novel's ending. Indeed, it is as much a struggle for Hawthorne to dispel the gloom of his narrative as it is for the Judge to disguise the "black" and "brooding" thundercloud of his temperament. The acute observer who probably suspected "that the smile on the gentleman's face was a good deal akin to the shine on his boots, and that each must have cost him and his boot-black, respectively, a good deal of hard labor to bring out and preserve them" (p. 117), might have said the same thing about the Judge's creator.

Perhaps even more ironic in this connection is Holgrave's—and Hawthorne's—volte-face on houses. When the daguerreotypist expresses a wish that the exterior of a house might differ from its interior, he unwittingly endorses a scheme of domestic architecture that has been practiced metaphorically by Jaffrey Pyncheon. It seems fitting, therefore, that he should take up residence in the Judge's elegant country seat rather than in the dwelling built by his ancestor, the house of the seven gables. Moreover, Hawthorne's house of fiction parallels the deceptive edifice of the Judge's being. Since a "devilish scowl would frighten away customers," as Dixey keeps insisting, he imposes a sunbathed conclusion on his narrative to cover up "the fearful secret, hidden within the house" (p. 291). Little wonder that the angry taunting of Jaffrey's corpse in chapter 18, "Governor Pyncheon," has struck many readers as excessive and slightly hysterical. It is not difficult to detect the self-reproach in Hawthorne's outbursts at the dead Judge for seeking profit and worldly honor and for wearing an "odious grin of feigned benignity, insolent in its pretense, and loathsome in its falsehood" (p. 282). Compelled by the pressures of the literary marketplace to "put on a bright face" for his readers, Hawthorne had become like the character whom he hated most in all his fiction.

When Holgrave reads Phoebe his story "Alice Pyncheon," and she is overcome by drowsiness, he remarks sarcastically on her "falling asleep at what I hoped the newspaper critics would pronounce a most brilliant, powerful, imaginative, pathetic, and original winding up!" (p. 212). With better reason, Hawthorne entertained a similar hope for the ending of his own story, and the newspaper critics responded by pronouncing *The House of the Seven Gables* a brilliant success, a book, as Whipple put it, in which "the humor and the pathos are combined." "Taken as a whole," Whipple added, "it is Hawthorne's greatest work, and is equally sure of immediate popularity and permanent fame." [21] Although in the long run sales lagged behind *The Scarlet Letter*, the new romance outsold its predecessor in the first year of publication and seemed to justify Hawthorne's decision (as he said of Hepzibah) to use the house of the seven gables as the setting of his commercial ventures. But that decision also seems to have intensified his negative feelings about the marketplace and its corrupting effect both on the writer as a producer and on the work of literature as a commodity. He wrote in the text that "a person of imaginative temperament," happening to pass the house of the seven gables on the morning after the summer storm, "would conceive the mansion to have been the residence of the stubborn old Puritan, Integrity, who, dying in some forgotten generation, had left a blessing in all its rooms and chambers, the efficacy of which was to be seen in the religion, honesty, moderate competence, or upright poverty, and solid happiness, of his descendants, to this day" (pp. 285–86). In an effort to obtain financial security from his writing—what he calls here a "moderate competence"—Hawthorne himself had built a literary mansion very different indeed from that inhabited by "Integrity." When he discovered soon enough that even his concession to the reader would not enable him to support his family, he may have come to feel as Hepzibah did after her first few hours behind the counter: that the enterprise "would prove [his] ruin, in a moral and religious point of view, without contributing very essentially towards even [his] temporal welfare" (p. 55). And while there were no doubt many causes for Hawthorne's "disintegration" as an artist,[22] *The House of the Seven Gables* suggests that his flagging energies were related to his growing alienation from the process of exchange.

6

Selling One's Head

Moby-Dick

I

In the third chapter of *Moby-Dick*, Melville's narrator Ishmael waits up anxiously for the arrival of the unknown harpooner with whom he is to share a bed. He feels misgivings about this arrangement— "No man prefers to sleep two in a bed"[1] (p. 41), he says—and his uneasiness turns into real apprehension when Peter Coffin, the Spouter Inn's landlord, observes that his overdue bedfellow has been delayed because "he can't sell his head." "Can't sell his head?" exclaims Ishmael:

> "Do you pretend to say, landlord, that this harpooner is actually engaged this blessed Saturday night, or rather Sunday morning, in peddling his head around this town?"
> "That's precisely it," said the landlord, "and I told him he couldn't sell it here, the market's overstocked."
> "With what?" shouted I.
> "With heads to be sure; ain't there too many heads in the world?" [Pp. 43–44]

Coffin clears up Ishmael's confusion by explaining that the harpooner has just arrived from the South Seas with a batch of embalmed aborigine heads, which he has been peddling as curios on the streets of New Bedford.

There may be better jokes in *Moby-Dick*, but this dialogue has the merit of wittily and unobtrusively specifying the novel's world as a thoroughly commercialized one. Out of the American realities of 1851, Melville creates a fictional setting where everything has become marketable and can be converted into money. Ishmael documents in exhaustive detail the production of sperm oil, but oil is only the most conspicuous of commodities in a book, where labor, heads, and even the "hills about Boston" (p. 549) are for sale. Indeed, Melville's subject is the commodity and its consequences. He depicts Ahab's hunt for the white whale as at once a revolt against and a corollary of a state of affairs, to borrow Emerson's phrase, in which "out of doors all seems a market."[2] As the author of the commodity *Moby-Dick*, Melville also probes the implications of the commercializing of literature. He holds two antithetical views of how to cope with the exchange relation to his readership. He oscillates between intimacy and absence as textual practices aimed at survival in a cultural environment where the writer has to sell his head.

II

The background to *Moby-Dick* is the critical juncture in American history when a fundamental reordering took place in men's relation to each other and their surroundings. "Are the green fields gone?" Ishmael asks as early as the third paragraph of his narrative (p. 24), and his question points to the moment of transition from an agricultural to a commercial and industrial society. (Later, in "A Bower in the Arsacides," Ishmael answers his own question in the affirmative when he imagines a textile mill materializing in the midst of the green woods.) Joint-stock ventures like the whaling industry set the pattern for a new economic order in which nature is systematically exploited for profit. Starbuck, the *Pequod*'s first mate, is the spokesman during the voyage for the commercial ethos of the age. "There's hogsheads of sperm ahead . . . ," he urges on his crewmen the first time the boats are lowered, "and that's what ye came for. (Pull, my boys!) Sperm, sperm's the play! This at least is duty; duty and profit hand in hand!" (p. 294). For Starbuck, the physical universe exists to be turned into merchandise and exchanged for dollars. Otherwise nature has no meaning for him, and he is incapable of understanding Ahab's feud with Moby Dick. During the quarterdeck scene, he objects that revenge is not worth pursuing because it has no exchange value: "I came here to hunt whales, not my commander's vengeance. How many barrels will thy vengeance yield thee even if thou gettest it, Captain Ahab? it will not fetch thee much in our Nantucket market" (p. 220).

Ahab's quest springs from a desire, to quote Emerson again, for "thoughts and principles not marketable."[3] He shares the Transcendentalist opposition to reducing nature to financial calculation. Whereas Starbuck and the ship's owners appreciate the world solely for its exchange value, Ahab sees a cosmos that pulsates with intelligent purpose, where every natural phenomenon is infused with spiritual significance. When the first mate appeals to the Nantucket market, Ahab replies that if the globe is to be computed into guineas, "one to every three parts of an inch," then his vengeance "will fetch a great premium *here*," striking his chest to indicate the incalculable value of inward gratification. Against money, he champions meaning as the only worthwhile goal. "All visible objects . . . ," he declares to Starbuck, "are but as pasteboard masks. But in each event—in the living act, the undoubted deed—there, some unknown but still reasoning thing puts forth the mouldings of its features from behind the unreasoning mask. If man will strike, strike through the mask!" (p. 220). In effect Ahab totally reverses the commercial assumptions of the shore. Rather than regarding commodification as conferring value on the universe, he believes that only a world vacant of value is fit to be bought and sold for money. Ishmael accurately conveys the Captain's viewpoint when he remarks, "some certain significance lurks in all things, else all things are little worth, and the round world itself but an empty cipher, except to sell by the cartload, as they do hills about Boston, to fill up some morass in the Milky Way" (p. 549).

Ahab's rebellion against the marketplace holds an extraordinarily powerful attraction for the *Pequod*'s crew. Although he himself uses the promise of cash to pacify the sailors, his principal appeal is based on uniting them in a purpose higher than financial remuneration. In some way he expresses a perception or grievance common to laboring men in the mid-nineteenth century. His quarrel with Moby Dick is an acknowledgment, however distorted and misplaced, of the alienated character of the commodity world. To Ahab, a potential article of exchange is in fact his deadly enemy. The white whale figures in his imagination, neither as a given amount of oil nor as "a dumb brute" attacking "from blindest instinct" (p. 220), but as a power that purposively threatens his existence. One might say that Ahab is like a factory worker, for just as the worker experiences his estranged labor, objectified in the commodity, as something "alien, hostile, powerful, and independent of him" (to quote Marx), so the *Pequod*'s captain views Moby Dick, a natural object convertible into money, as willful and inimical to his interests.[4] Of course Ahab and the sailors are not factory workers, although in "The Try-Works" chapter Melville gives a vivid picture of the manufacturing stage of whaling, implicitly associating the *Pequod*'s voyage with the industrial phase of capitalist development.[5] The estrangement Ahab feels from the commodity world, his conviction that it is antagonistic to his welfare, is a response to conditions which if relatively new are nevertheless becoming characteristic of antebellum American society. His enraged reaction to an alienated reality is surely part of what enables him to gain ascendancy over the whalemen. Every member of the crew, with the partial exception of Starbuck, is won over to his fiery quest. The sailors respond so instinctively to Ahab's mission that, in Ishmael's words, "his hate seemed almost theirs; the White Whale as much their insufferable foe as his" (p. 251).

In waging war against Moby Dick, Ahab is not simply attacking the commodity form; he is also attempting, in the manner of Emerson, to overcome alienation and reclaim the world for man. "Not the smallest atom stirs or lives on matter," believes the *Pequod*'s captain, "but has its cunning duplicate in mind" (p. 406). He insists that signification can be found everywhere in the physical environment, and meaning is something to which men can relate even if the meaning in question is malign. The nonhuman world, as embodied in the white whale, may appear evil and antagonistic to Ahab, but for just this reason it is not completely alien. It is an emblematic language which men can decipher and respond to, a communication from a natural or supernatural source. Ahab's symbolic mode of perception seeks to defeat alienation by replacing a world degraded into dollars with a cosmos where intelligible messages inhere in the structure of things.

To Melville, Ahab's strategy for humanizing nature is a failure. It fails most obviously because whales in general, and the white whale in particular, frustrate the effort to discover their objective meaning. Throughout his narrative, Ishmael strives to find the "certain significance" supposedly lurking in every natural fact, but his studies yield only the conclusion that the whale eludes his understanding. For each part of the anatomy that he investigates, he is forced to confess his bafflement: "The more I consider this mighty tail, the more do I deplore my inability to express it. At times there are gestures in it, which, though they would well grace the hand of a man, remain wholly inexplicable. . . . Dissect him now I may, then, I go but skin deep; I know him not, and never will" (p. 486). Moby Dick remains similarly inscrutable, his behavior neither confirming or disproving Ahab's interpretation of him as malicious.

A second reason for questioning Ahab's project is that, in construing Moby Dick as a symbol rather than a commodity, he participates in the very way of thinking he opposes. He is as much involved in an exchange process as his former shipmates, the *Pequod*'s owners, only in his case he converts objects not into money but into meaning. Like the marketplace, which honors things for their cash value, he ignores nature's uses and beauty in order to focus on what it represents. Chapter 99, "The Doubloon," develops the equivalence between monetary and symbolic transactions, underscoring Ahab's connivance in the system of exchange. As currency, the doubloon can buy an infinite variety of items (Flask, for example, would like to spend it for nine hundred and sixty cigars); as a physical object with inscriptions, it elicits an infinite number of interpretations. The sailors who pore over the coin's meaning do in the realm of thought what money enables them to do in the commodity realm.[6]

Ahab's Emersonian program for vanquishing the market fails, finally, because it replicates the essence of alienation: it suppresses or mystifies the human element in the production of meaning. Just as man's labor appears to have vanished from the commodity, so the signification that Ahab attributes to objects is not of human making. Moby Dick's malevolence, he maintains in his quarterdeck speech, is an objective fact, a reality out there in the material universe. It exists independently of anything he may think or do. Yet Melville leaves little doubt that Ahab's conception of the whale is generated out of his own subjectivity. As Ishmael observes, the Captain "came to identify with [Moby Dick], not only all his bodily woes, but all his intellectual and spiritual exasperations. . . . He piled upon the whale's white hump the sum of all the general rage and hate felt by his whole race from Adam down" (pp. 246–47). At one point in "The Doubloon" even Ahab realizes that he has been projecting his personal attitudes onto nature. Pausing before the gold coin, he admits that each understanding of its figures reflects the individual observer: "The firm tower, that is Ahab; the volcano, that is Ahab; the courageous, the undaunted, and victorious fowl, that, too, is Ahab; all are Ahab; and this round gold is but the image of the rounder globe, which, like a magician's glass, to each and every man in turn but mirrors back his own mysterious self" (p. 551). Ishmael's narrative bears out neither Ahab's vision of the globe nor that of any other character, but it does vindicate an insight implicit in the Captain's statement: all meanings are created by human beings.

III

Along with the manufacture and sale of sperm oil, Melville is concerned with the composition and exchange of texts. He seeks to understand the writer's status as a maker of commodities and to explore how this condition might affect the literary artifact. At times his dissatisfaction with the dehumanizing nature of market relations is unmistakable. He challenges the illusion of impersonality in literature and tries to restore awareness of the human agent in the production both of books and of social reality. Yet Melville is anything but consistent in his attitude toward the reading public. His use of Ishmael as a first-person narrator and his way of relating the story reveal a basic indecision in his aesthetic strategy. Ishmael is a disguise, a fictional persona, but he is also a vehicle for Melville's own thoughts and feelings. It would be as mistaken to conflate him with his creator as to deny the identity between them. The ambiguity built into the character of Ishmael manifests itself most strikingly in the flagrant inconsistency of point of view. The narrative alternates between direct address and suppression of the personal voice, issuing at times from a flesh-and-blood figure who participates in the action, and at other times from a disembodied intelligence that appears to possess omniscience. Hence the narrative suggests not merely Melville's wish to repudiate the commodity form but his complicity in a social and economic order where men relate as things—embalmed and shrunken heads—instead of as human beings.

This immense novel about the whaling industry delights in showing how goods are made, literary wares included. At the book's heart is the elaborately described process whereby a living part of nature is transformed into an object of human consumption. Hundreds of pages of dense and often technically detailed prose are devoted to the fashioning of a commodity; the climactic battle with Moby Dick, by contrast, gets a scant three chapters out of a hundred and thirty-five. Ishmael relates—or rather sings, to adopt his own word—how the great leviathan is sighted from the masthead and slaughtered on the deep; "how he is then towed alongside and beheaded; and how . . . his great padded partout becomes the property of his executioner; how, in due time, he is condemned to the pots . . . ;" and how his oil is decanted into casks and finally stowed in the hold (p. 545). At each step of this extended process the reader is shown working men carrying out the operation of turning nature into merchandise. If *Moby-Dick* is a commercial epic, it is an epic much like *Walden* in which human labor is not marginalized but situated at the center.[7]

As with sperm oil, so with literature. Melville strives to overcome the dehumanizing effects of commodification on narrative. He is at pains to associate the act of writing with the business of whaling, and to place his own activity as an author as much before the reader as that of the crew. Just as the sailors change the leviathan into a consumable item, so Ishmael proposes to fashion the monster into a text. In the "Cetology" chapter he announces his ambition to compile a history of the sperm whale. "As yet . . . ," he says, "the sperm whale, scientific or poetic, lives not complete in any literature. Far above all other hunted whales, his is an unwritten life" (p. 181). He proceeds to sketch out a plan of classification for whales in general and to enumerate the distinguishing characteristics of the various species. His cetological or "Bibliographical system" (p. 188) underlines the parallel between whales and works of literature. He arranges the creatures according to magnitude and groups them under terms used in printing to refer to book size, labeling the largest whales "Folio," the next in order "Octavo," and the smallest "Duodecimo." He then subdivides the books themselves into chapters, so that representative headings read as follows: "BOOK I. (*Folio*), Chapter I. (*Sperm Whale*)," "BOOK III. (*Duodecimo*), Chapter II (*Algerine Porpoise*)."[8]

Repeatedly Ishmael directs the reader's attention to the labor involved in making literature out of "The Whale" (the subtitle of *Moby-Dick*). It is an arduous task, he claims, and "no ordinary letter-sorter in the Post-Office is equal to it. . . . But I have swam through libraries and sailed through oceans; I have had to do with whales with these visible hands; I am in earnest; and I will try" (pp. 181–82). His literary project requires him to assimilate vast quantities of scientific and historical information and to familiarize himself with naturalists from antiquity to the present. Throughout the narrative he displays his scholarly researches by invoking, disputing, and correcting the leading authorities on whaling. He makes no effort to conceal the mechanics of literary production. As he busily goes about assembling his material, he constantly reminds his readers of the man-madeness of the object before them.

Indeed, the visibility of its making is one of the most arresting features of *Moby-Dick* as an aesthetic performance. Ishmael often pauses in the midst of his descriptions to alert the reader to what he is doing and explain the reasons for his decisions. He lets the customer into his workshop, as it were, and opens the creative process before him.[9] Ishmael might say, for example, that a particular passage is necessary to prepare for subsequent actions or to establish "the reasonableness of the whole story of the White Whale, more especially the catastrophe" (p. 276). Typical is the sentence which introduces chapter 60, "The Line": "With reference to the whaling scene shortly to be described, as well as for the better understanding of all similar scenes elsewhere presented, I have here to speak of the magical, sometimes horrible whale-line" (p. 368). Ishmael is equally forthcoming about characterization. Portraying himself as a tragic dramatist, he freely confides to his audience the difficulty of writing tragedy about a common mariner such as Ahab: "I must not conceal that I have only to do with a poor old whale-hunter like him; and, therefore, all outward and majestical trappings and housings are denied me" (p. 199). Ishmael's candor about technique has the effect of diminishing alienation by showing the human agent engaged in the construction of the artwork.

Ishmael—or rather Melville—also makes his artistic activity perceptible by bringing together an array of different literary forms within a single volume. *Moby-Dick* incorporates elements of the dictionary (the "Etymology"), of an encyclopedia (the "Extracts"), and of an anatomy (the speculations on free will or Ishmael's meditation in "The Mast-Head"); it includes sermons, soliloquies, and a short story. There is no attempt to pretend that fiction is an objective transcription of reality. Melville's effort is not to disguise form but to assert it, not to aim for translucency but to emphasize the artificiality of his writing. He wants to interpose himself between the reader and what the reader sees, rather than to create the impression of things or scenes appearing to view without the intervention of a constructing hand. His sensibility in exhibiting his fabrication of the text is closer to that of the artisan than that of the industrial worker. *Moby-Dick* implies a connection between the realist goal of providing a transparent window on the actual and the effacing of the maker from the commodity form. As Walter Benjamin has pointed out, the hand once played a central role in narration just as it did in production; it enhanced the speaker's performance by supporting his words with gestures.[10] Ishmael said that he had "had to do with whales with these visible hands"; Melville allies himself with the artisanal tradition of storytelling by trying to make his hands as visible as he can.[11]

It is not only the concealment of the producer that Melville wishes to avert; it is also the depersonalizing of the reader, the buyer of his books. He invites his audience into the text, not simply to show them how it is put together, but to elicit their involvement in its creation.[12] Once again, the analogy to the artisan or craftsman is illuminating. The artisan impresses his personal stamp upon the product of his labor, which is commonly made according to the specifications of the customer. With the commodity the buyer loses his active role in production; he has contributed nothing of himself to the object he purchases.[13] In *Moby-Dick* Ishmael's style of narration is very much in the artisanal or storyteller's mode. The direct addresses—beginning with the celebrated imperative, "Call me Ishmael" (p. 23)—the rhetorical questions, the admonitions, the frequent use of the present tense to comment on the action and point the moral, and the prevailing chattiness—all convey a sense of interaction with the audience.

Ishmael's emphasis on the reader's participation also has to do with the spirit of mutuality springing from commerce generally. Capitalist enterprises such as whaling did not preclude positive interaction between individuals, and the resulting "mortal inter-indebtedness" (p. 601), in Ahab's phrase, becomes paradigmatic for the relation between writer and reader. The sailors who produce the sperm oil work in concert rather than alone, and the physical experience of life on the whaler encourages an ethic of cooperation. Chapter 72, "The Monkey-Rope," dramatizes this point. During the cutting-in operation, while Queequeg flounders about on the back of a half-submerged whale, Ishmael keeps his friend from going under by managing a line of hemp tied to both their waists. The two men are for a time as closely bound to each other as Siamese twins: should the cannibal drown, the monkey-rope would drag Ishmael down in his wake. This situation leads Melville's narrator to reflect on the limits of personal autonomy:

> I seemed distinctly to perceive that my own individuality was now merged in a joint stock company of two: that my free will had received a mortal blow; and that another's mistake or misfortune might plunge innocent me into unmerited disaster and death. . . . I saw that this situation of mine was the precise situation of every mortal that breathes; only, in most cases, he,

one way or other, has this Siamese connexion with a plurality of other mortals. If your banker breaks, you snap; if your apothecary by mistake sends you poison in your pills, you die. [P. 416]

Ishmael's generality about the human fate arises from the specific kinds of interdependence which occur in commercial civilization. The trope, "joint stock company of two," encapsulates the idea that commerce can foster a sense of trust and mutual responsibility. While the perils of the monkey-rope are undeniably real, so are the feelings of affection which strongly color this episode, causing Ishmael to call Queequeg his "dear comrade and twin-brother" (p. 417). Or as he says elsewhere, imagining Queequeg's unspoken thoughts, "It's a mutual, joint-stock world, in all meridians. We cannibals must help these Christians" (p. 96).

Ishmael establishes a monkey-rope bond with the reader by constantly appealing for support, offering assistance, or joining forces to solve a problem. His demand for participation turns the text into a "joint stock company of two." The "I"-"you" relation of the opening sentence becomes a partnership in which "we" share a common interest in comprehending the whale. "Can we . . . hope to light upon some chance clue to conduct us to the hidden cause we seek?" asks Ishmael about the mystery of whiteness, adding, "Let us try" (p. 259). His inquiries commonly begin with an invitation—"Let us, then, look at this matter" (p. 475)—and end with a collaborative statement such as "thus we see" (p. 579) or "we must conclude" (p. 585). He is solicitous to prevent misunderstanding, and if he feels that an explanation has failed to satisfy, he will volunteer, "I have another idea for you" (p. 451), or interject, "Explain thyself, Ishmael" (p. 571). As a helpful gesture, he supplements the body of his narrative with footnotes on matters as various as the albatross (p. 256), the verb "to gally" (p. 493), and the method for detecting leakage in oil casks (p. 602). He expects the reader's cooperation in return, noting in his disquisition on whiteness that "without imagination no man can follow another into these halls" (p. 259). When he is about to examine the heads of a sperm whale and a right whale, he remarks, "Here, now, are two great whales, laying their heads together; let us join them, and lay together our own" (p. 427). The second mate Stubb, trying to decode the engravings on the doubloon, furnishes a gloss on the kind of collaborative effort called for by Ishmael's narrative: "Book! you lie there; the fact is, you books must know your places.

You'll do to give us the bare words and facts, but we come in to supply the thoughts" (p. 553).

In urging his readers to enter the text and share in its making, Melville honors the human connection dissolved in the commodity and offers an alternative to Ahab's assertion of metaphysical significance. He shows that meaning emerges from social interaction. Within the novel itself, "The Town-Ho's Story" gives an illustration of the author-audience involvement Melville desires. This chapter carries the subtitle "As told at the Golden Inn" (p. 321), and Ishmael appears in it as a storyteller engaged in convivial give-and-take with an attentive gathering of listeners. "For my humor's sake," he says of the story, "I shall preserve the style in which I once narrated it at Lima, to a lounging circle of my Spanish friends, one saint's eve, smoking upon the thick-gilt tiled piazza of the Golden Inn" (p. 322). As he gets into the narrative, the cavaliers regularly interrupt to put questions, refill his cup, and contribute observations of their own. Ishmael's replies are included along with their comments, and the story acquires its shape as a common enterprise, the product of a relation between persons. There is only one uncomfortable moment, which occurs at the end of the chapter: Ishmael's auditors are unable to repress their skepticism about the truth of his story, and he requests a copy of the Gospels in order to swear to its veracity.

IV

"Try to get a living by the Truth," Melville exclaimed to Hawthorne while hard at work on *Moby-Dick*, "and go to the Soup Societies." The frustration, perhaps the anger, in this remark points to an aspect of the novel at odds with Ishmael's sociability, a counterpressure to the friendliness of the raconteur which stems from Melville's realistic assessment of the economics of authorship. Having enlarged and substantially rewritten his work-in-progress, Melville fell behind schedule in delivering the manuscript to his publishers and was driven to ask for a new advance; when his request was refused, he had to borrow two thousand dollars (a sizable sum then) to enable him to support his family. He had no intention of falsifying his art but neither did he wish to end up in the poorhouse with his infant son and pregnant wife. He was determined to complete the book quickly and was understandably anxious for a success. As he poured out his frustration to Hawthorne, he dwelt on the conflict between his devotion to the truth and his financial necessities:

The calm, the coolness, the silent grass-growing mood in which a man *ought* always to compose,—that, I fear, can seldom be mine. Dollars damn me; and the malicious Devil is forever grinning in upon me, holding the door ajar. My dear Sir, a presentiment is on me,—I shall at last be worn out and perish, like an old nutmeg-grater, grated to pieces by the constant attrition of the wood, that is, the nutmeg. What I feel most moved to write, that is banned,—it will not pay. Yet, altogether, write the *other* way I cannot. So the product is a final hash, and all my books are botches.[14]

For Melville, even a work as creatively involving as *Moby-Dick* was inevitably compromised by the pressures of the literary marketplace. The need to sell imposed a restraint on the degree of self-expression he could permit himself. Two years earlier, speaking of *Redburn* and *White-Jacket* in a letter to his father-in-law, Melville portrayed himself as a workman compelled to tailor his fiction to the demands of buyers. Describing the two novels as concessions to popular taste, he tried to dissociate himself from them as not issuing from his deepest feelings:

No reputation that is gratifying to me, can possibly be achieved by either of these books. They are two *jobs*, which I have done for money—being forced to it, as other men are to sawing wood. . . . I have felt obliged to refrain from writing the kind of book I would wish. . . . Being books, then, written in this way, my only desire for their "success" (as it is called) springs from my pocket, and not from my heart.

If monetary considerations could be put aside, Melville continued, his preference would be to write the sort of books which are regarded as failures.[15]

Moby-Dick was written from the heart, but it was hardly independent of the pocket: Melville could no more afford a book that failed in 1851 than in 1849. He was obviously still subject to the pressures that caused him to feel displeased with *Redburn* and *White-Jacket*. There are indications throughout *Moby-Dick* of his estrangement from both his art and his readers. To produce to satisfy consumers is, for Melville, necessarily to efface one's individuality; it is to be in a position analogous to the laborer hired by employers. In the letter to his father-in-law, he likened writing to sawing wood, and among the characters aboard the *Pequod* is a carpenter whose complaints are re-

minders of this comparison.[16] The carpenter objects to being forced
to fashion a life-buoy out of Queequeg's coffin. "Are all my pains to
go for nothing with that coffin?" grumbles this self-portrait of the
artist, voicing Melville's irritation at having to revise his novel to conform to others' expectations. "And now I'm ordered to make a life-
buoy of it. It's like turning an old coat; going to bring the flesh on
the other side now. I don't like this cobbling sort of business—I
don't like it at all; it's undignified; it's not my place." In the carpenter's
alienation from the product of his labor, one senses Melville's own
disaffection from the text as commodity, an object produced for sale
on the market. "We workers in woods make bridal-bedsteads and
card-tables, as well as coffins and hearses. We work by the month, or
by the job, or by the profit; not for us to ask the why and wherefore
of our work, unless it be too confounded cobbling, and then we stash
it if we can" (pp. 663–64).

In his piece on Hawthorne, Melville drew two inferences from the
commodity status of fiction: he cautioned against telling the truth
openly in the marketplace, because to do so risked offending one's
audience, and he proposed the idea of the absent author or foundling
text as a response to the necessity for self-concealment. In *Moby-Dick*,
he introduces the problem of audience rejection in Father Mapple's
sermon on Jonah. Mapple's subject is the difficulty of preaching the
truth in a world of falsehood, and he describes how Jonah, "being a
pilot-prophet or speaker of true things, and bidden by the Lord to
sound those unwelcome truths in the ears of a wicked Nineveh," fled
from his duty because he was "appalled at the hostility he should
raise" (p. 79). Melville had many reasons to fear a hostile reaction to
his novel: its critical view of America,[17] its advocacy of interracial
brotherhood,[18] its lack of cosmic optimism[19]—on these and other
grounds he would have identified with Jonah and felt the need to distance himself from the public.[20]

Melville's portrayal of Father Mapple and the worshipers at the
Whaleman's Chapel amounts to an alternative version of artist-
audience relations, a version, in contrast to "The Town-Ho's Story,"
where the emphasis falls on withdrawal and isolation rather than fellowship. Mapple physically cuts himself off from his congregation,
ascending to a high pulpit by means of a rope ladder which he draws
up behind him. Not a word of dialogue is exchanged between the
minister and his parishioners, who listen to the sermon in silence and
seem "purposely sitting apart" from each other, "insular and in-
communicable" (p. 63). At the end of the service they file out with-

out speaking, while Mapple remains kneeling with his face in his hands, "till all the people had departed, and he was left alone in the place" (p. 81).

The separation between Mapple and his audience is both criticized and reproduced in Melville's manner of writing the novel. Ishmael's face-to-face overtures coexist with a tendency toward authorial withdrawal, as Melville shows himself to be of two minds about the possibility of humanizing the work of literature as commodity. If he reveals the fabricating hand, he also shields the human face behind a mask of objectivity, as though to acknowledge as inescapable the loss of the person in exchange. The living speech of the storyteller vies with "the death of the author,"[21] resulting in the disappearance of the first-person voice from whole stretches of the narrative. Moreover, the first-person speaker is himself a more guarded and elusive figure than his air of sociability suggests. Even his opening salutation reflects a wish for anonymity as well as for companionship. In asking to be called Ishmael, he comes before the reader not "in his own proper character" but under a biblical pseudonym that expresses his sense of alienation.[22]

The desire to orphan the text, to sunder it from an identifiable parent or producer, is as marked in *Moby-Dick* as the willingness to exhibit its manufacture. Although Ishmael puts his scholarly labors on display, he seems curiously reluctant to impress his individual point of view upon "The Whale." He introduces himself in the role of an editor, the compiler of pages of "Extracts" on whales, and as he continues to quote sources as diverse as Job, Linnaeus, and Owen Chase, his particular voice merges into the clamor of voices belonging to those who have "thought, fancied, and sung of Leviathan" (p. 7). His intention, Ishmael states in giving examples of the sperm whale's ferocity, is to allow the material to speak for itself: "I care not to perform . . . my task methodically; but shall be content to produce the desired impression by separate citations of items, practically or reliably known to me as a whaleman; and from these citations, I take it—the conclusion aimed at will naturally follow of itself" (p. 273). When he finds available conceptions inadequate, he often refuses to venture his own alternative. In chapter 55, for example, which describes erroneous pictures of the whale, he begins by vowing "ere long to paint . . . as well as one can without canvas, something like the true form of the whale as he actually appears to the eye" (p. 346). But by the end of the chapter, he has reached the position that "the great Leviathan is that one creature in the world which must remain unpainted to the last . . . there is no earthly way of finding out precisely what the whale really looks like" (p. 352).

Ishmael's strong interest in seeing things from as many angles as possible further contributes to the impression of authorial removal. He scrutinizes the whale from every imaginable point of view: scientific, mythological, legal, historical, religious, political, and literary. The difference between his approach and Ahab's single-minded one is illustrated by "The Whiteness of the Whale," where he investigates the color white in its myriad forms and finds it to be "at once the most meaning symbol of spiritual things, nay, the very veil of the Christian's Deity; and . . . the intensifying agent in things the most appalling to mankind" (p. 263). Ishmael's determination to entertain incompatible opinions leads him to efface his subjectivity so that he appears to lack a discernible perspective. Contemplating the whale's spout, he keeps revising and reversing his position until no judgment seems preferable to any other:

> how can you certainly tell whether any water falls from it, when, always, when you are close enough to a whale to get a close view of his spout, he is in a prodigious commotion, the water cascading all around him. And if at such times you should think that you really perceived drops of moisture in the spout, how do you know that they are not merely condensed from its vapor; or how do you know that they are not those identical drops superficially lodged in the spout-hole fissure, which is countersunk into the summit of the whale's head?
> [P. 479]

"The Doubloon" shows how Ishmael's adoption of multiple perspectives results not merely in the blurring of his individual viewpoint but in the vanishing of a definable narrative consciousness. As the sailors pass before the coin trying to interpret its writing, the narrative voice undergoes a succession of changes. Ishmael introduces the chapter, Ahab follows with a soliloquy, and he in turn is followed by an omniscient narrator who describes Starbuck and Stubb speaking to themselves. Stubb is apparently the next narrator, since he overhears Flask's reflections ("here comes little King-Post; dodge round the tryworks, now, and let's hear what he'll have to say" [p. 554]), but then Stubb disappears and Flask reports on Queequeg's motions before the coin ("What says the Cannibal? As I live, he's comparing notes; looking at his thigh bone; thinks the sun is in the thigh, or in the calf, or in the bowels" [p. 555]). The third mate continues to eavesdrop while Pip comes forward and conjugates the verb "to look," whereupon he also disappears ("So, so, I leave him muttering" [p. 556]), and the omniscient narrator returns to relate Pip's final monologue.

Moby-Dick is "The Doubloon" writ large. As Ishmael appears, fades from sight, and reappears, Melville's novel gives the impression of being an object without a single, originating maker. The book starts off as a relatively straightforward first-person chronicle, with Ishmael as teller and central character. But once the *Pequod* sets sail, the young man yields his protagonist's role to Ahab and has to share his literary duties with a more experienced whaleman. This figure, an expert on cetology, still uses the first-person singular and is presumably an older version of Ishmael. He proves as dispensable as his youthful self, giving way at times to the omniscient voice that is first heard in chapter 29, "Enter Ahab; to Him, Stubb."

As the title of chapter 29 indicates, Melville experiments with writing *Moby-Dick* in the dramatic mode and eliminating the narrative persona altogether. The theatrical devices, which include soliloquies and asides as well as stage directions, reveal the pervasive influence of Shakespeare; there are allusions and borrowings from *Macbeth*, *Hamlet*, and *King Lear*. The playwright is Melville's model for the absent truth-teller, and in the dramatic chapters he follows Shakespeare's example by abolishing all traces of Ishmael's presence. He reports episodes and conversations, such as those in chapter 109, "Ahab and Starbuck in the Cabin," to which neither of the "I's" supposedly telling the story could have had access. Even scenes Ishmael claims to have taken part in, like the gathering on the quarterdeck, are described from a third-person perspective, as though being observed on a stage. ("The Quarter-Deck" is subtitled "Enter Ahab: Then, all.") Still other chapters contain no narrative voice at all. Chapters 37 and 38, "Sunset" and "Dusk," consist entirely of stage directions and interior monologues, and chapter 40, "Midnight, Forecastle," is presented like a scene from a play, with each speaker's name printed above his dialogue. One has no sense that Ishmael—or indeed, anyone—has written these pages; lacking a mediating point of view, they produce the illusion of a text without an author.

The commodifying of literature, then, drives Melville to remove himself from sections of *Moby-Dick*. This seeming authorlessness is a technical device for which there are thematic or psychological correlatives. Counterbalancing Ishmael's affable storytelling is his extensive concern with death. The ultimate disappearance of the narrator would mean his demise, and from the first paragraph of his tale Ishmael shows a morbid fascination with coffins, funerals, and dying. While his friendship with Queequeg cures him of the wish to commit suicide, he remains preoccupied as a teller with the appeal of personal extinction. "If, at my death," he writes, "my executors, or more properly my creditors, find any precious MSS. in my desk, then here I prospectively ascribe all the honor and glory to whaling" (p. 156). A posthumous manuscript, having no surviving parent, would be a literary foundling. According to Ishmael, it would have the power to communicate truths beyond the grasp of any living writer: "the drawing near of Death, which alike levels all, alike impresses all with a last revelation, which only an author from the dead could adequately tell" (p. 608). In a related passage, Melville's narrator suggests that the answers to the deepest riddles of man's being have to be sought in the grave:

> Where lies the final harbor, whence we unmoor no more? In what rapt ether sails the world, of which the weariest will never weary? Where is the foundling's father hidden? Our souls are like those orphans whose unwedded mothers die in bearing them: the secret of our paternity lies in their grave, and we must there to learn it. [P. 624]

Melville's novel was published simultaneously in London and New York, and the English edition realizes his idea of a story without a teller, a book "by an author from the dead." *Moby-Dick* appeared in England without the "Epilogue," every member of the *Pequod*'s crew apparently having sunk with the ship. "The Whale" thus becomes a commodity from which the human source has been eradicated. To critics like the reviewer for *The Spectator*, Melville was guilty of transgressing the most fundamental rules of fiction writing. "Nothing should be introduced into a novel which it is physically impossible for the writer to have known: thus, he must not describe the conversation of miners in a pit if they *all* perish."[23] It is not clear whether Melville added the final two paragraphs, preceded by the words from the book of Job, "And I only am escaped alone to tell thee" (p. 723), as a concession to his American publishers, or whether they were misplaced when he mailed the proofs to England. Perhaps, anticipating probable criticism, he intended to include them all along. In any case, the "Epilogue," though permitting Ishmael to survive the wreck, retains the spirit of the English edition. The means of Ishmael's escape from an ocean grave is a coffin, and the last words he utters re-affirm his identity as an orphan: "It was the devious-cruising Rachel, that in her retracing search after her missing children, only found an-other orphan" (p. 724).

V

In its equivocal reaction to the literary work as an article of com-merce, Melville's masterpiece recalls *The Scarlet Letter*. *Moby-Dick* is dedicated to Hawthorne, and although the two writers differ aes-thetically as much as they do temperamentally, both reveal in their fiction a split between the wish to connect with the public and the belief that to "speak in the marketplace," the artist has to absent him-self from his readers, whether by employing deception or by retiring into impersonality. The confusion in Melville's novel between first-person and omniscient narration expresses that fissuring and evokes the similar, if more orderly, division in *The Scarlet Letter* between Hawthorne's account of his stint in the customhouse and his history of Hester and Arthur. Perhaps an even better analogy is with the un-explained change of voice in Dimmesdale's dying confession. In both books there is an association of writing or speech with death: Haw-thorne claims to be writing "from beyond the grave," and Melville's narrator Ishmael, declaring "I survived myself" (p. 304), is given a reprieve from drowning to tell the truth known only to the dead. Both writers are drawn to the idea of the missing or absent parent, in part for reasons of personal history, but also because of their ap-prehensions about being "found out" in their fiction.

The surest method of avoiding detection in a work of art, and of achieving absence as an author, is not to write at all. "Seldom have I known any profound being that had anything to say to this world," Ishmael observes at one point about the whale's silence, "unless forced to stammer out something by way of getting a living" (p. 478). For Ishmael's creator, the objectives of "getting a living" and saying what is on his mind prove impossible to unify. The contradictory at-titudes toward exchange that Melville shares with the Hawthorne of *The Scarlet Letter* develop into the almost total alienation of his later work and eventuate in his decision to abjure the novel. The linking of death and writing in *Moby-Dick* contains the germ of this develop-ment and is to receive unforgettable expression in the "dead letters" of "Bartleby, the Scrivener."[24] The same association helps to illumi-nate the disillusionment with literature, or more precisely prose narrative, that has prompted critics to speak of "Melville's quarrel with fiction." [25] Letters of death, from which the writer has succeeded in absenting himself, would be truly alienated commodities. Their producer would experience such texts as having no connection to himself. To put it in Ishmael's terms, they would appear to him as "empty ciphers." Ahab, we know, reacts with outrage to this situation: turning against the commodity world, he comes to see the white whale as his enemy. By revolting against not only his readers but his writing, Melville joins the crewmen of the *Pequod* in following the lead of his greatest character: the novel becomes his Moby Dick.

7

"Bartleby, the Scrivener" and the Transformation of the Economy

Bartleby, the Scrivener, A Story of Wall Street" shares with *Moby-Dick* a concern with illegibility, focusing as does the novel on an object that proves inaccessible to understanding. In *Moby-Dick* the inscrutable object is natural, the great white whale pursued by Ahab; in "Bartleby" it is social, a human being who belongs to a different class from that of the narrator and Melville's readers. What interests Melville in the story is not so much the fact of inaccessibility as what lies behind it, the growing distance between the classes which relegates men like Bartleby to invisibility and makes comprehension of them unlikely if not impossible in capitalist America. "Bartleby" is a story about class relations and their consequences; as such, it is also an investigation into the narrative's own unintelligibility to the reader.

"A Story of Wall Street" is Melville's significant subtitle, and Wall Street, as the financial hub of American capitalism, is the center from which radiate the many walls dividing society and segregating its members. Walls and barriers figure prominently throughout "Bartleby": the lawyer's office is surrounded by walls, and Bartleby, once he ceases copying, spends all his time in a "dead-wall revery" (p. 59).[1] Within the office there are walls as well, the lawyer having arranged ground-glass folding doors so as to divide his premises into two sections, "one of which was occupied by my scriveners, the other by myself" (p. 46). The lawyer-narrator further procures "a high green folding screen" behind which he places Bartleby in order to "isolate [him] from my sight, though not remove him from my voice" (p. 46). The effect of these partitions is to separate the office into a series of cells, anticipating Bartleby's eventual immurement in the Tombs and suggesting that for the scriveners and their employer everyday life has come to resemble life inside a prison.[2]

In many ways, of course, this particular office seems far too cozy and humorous to be thought of as a prison. Melville deliberately creates an atmosphere reminiscent of Charles Dickens's *A Christmas Carol*, published a decade earlier,[3] and his narrator's prefatory remarks evoke the affectionate familiarity between the classes which was often presented as an ideal in British fiction of the period. The lawyer's chambers at No. —— Wall Street have a distinctly English flavor: Turkey and Nippers are Englishmen in point of fact, and the narrator's paternalistic attitude toward them seems more appropriate to the antiquated, vaguely feudal world of masters and servants than to the actual working conditions emerging in mid-nineteenth-century America. Indeed, at the time when the story takes place the lawyer has just received "the Master's office" (p. 45), a reference to the since abolished office of Master in Chancery but also an accurate description of his sense of his position.[4] In keeping with the hierarchical structure of master-servant relations, he wants his subordinates to know their own place as well as to show respect to him; hence while he disapproves of Nippers's "diseased ambition," he has high praise for Turkey's "natural civility and deference, as a dependent Englishman" (pp. 43–44). Yet for the most part the lawyer's attitude is marked by tolerance and not severity. He cheerfully puts up with his employees' eccentricities and even organizes his work day to accommodate their fits of inefficiency. And he tends to think of them in personal terms rather than in terms of money: aware that Turkey is unable to afford a new coat, for example, the narrator presents the threadbare scrivener with "a highly respectable-looking coat of my own" (p. 44), responding with an act of charity instead of an offer to increase his wages.

Perhaps the key point about the narrator, as he reveals in the story's opening sentence, is his age. "I am a rather elderly man," he announces in introducing himself to the reader, and he goes on to report with pride that he was once employed by "the late John Jacob Astor," the merchant capitalist who made a fortune in the fur trade at the beginning of the nineteenth century (pp. 39–40). The importance of such details is that they establish the lawyer as having formed his economic views in an earlier stage of capitalist development; in certain respects he literally does belong to the world of masters and servants, or at least masters and apprentices—to a regime, in other words, that was rapidly becoming obsolete by 1853, when Melville composed his "Story of Wall Street." Apprenticeship arrangements, it is true, still obtained in the legal profession, and the youngster known as Ginger Nut has been placed with the narrator expressly to acquire training in the law. But in the economy as a whole the old order of face-to-face contacts and mutual obligations was steadily giving way to the impersonal calculus of the market.

In America the regime of mutuality had been associated with the household system. Workmen had commonly served terms of apprenticeship, often in their own homes or those of neighbors, to prepare them to become self-supporting artisans. The rationalization and growth of capitalist enterprise in the middle decades of the century turned many of these once independent workmen into wage-earning proletarians and established cash payment as the sole nexus between employer and employee. Obligations, generally between strangers, were now purely contractual, and traditional habits of sociability yielded to a new emphasis on regularity and discipline.[5]

This is to say that the erosion of the household system was accompanied by a more rigorous, profit-seeking ethos on the part of capital. And here too Melville's narrator retains the less aggressive outlook of the past. Though he admires Astor profusely, he himself has none of the millionaire's energy and little of his single-minded acquisitiveness. In a profession proverbially enterprising, he is "one of those unambitious lawyers who never address a jury, or in any way draw down public applause; but, in the cool tranquillity of a snug retreat, do a snug business among rich men's bonds, and mortgages, and title-deeds." A notably cautious figure, he boasts of his prudence and is quite vain of his reputation as "an eminently *safe* man" (p. 40).

While Melville recognizes the appealing features of the narrator's Dickensian office, he does not idealize it, nor is he uncritical of the outmoded economic attitude it represents. On the contrary, he treats the office with considerable irony, leaving no doubt of the lawyer's failure to accord his three subordinates their full humanity. Turkey, Nippers, and Ginger Nut appear in the lawyer's narrative as caricatures; however good-natured, his portraits of them effectively reduce them to their "humors," as if they were partial or mechanical men. Even their names are indicative of their diminished humanity, for in fact he never identifies them by their real names but only by the condescending nicknames which supposedly express their personalities. The lawyer's paternalism simply precludes any acknowledgment of his employees' autonomy. His act of charity is symptomatic of his shortcomings. Giving Turkey a secondhand coat may have the virtues of a personal gesture, but unlike higher wages, which are earned, it assumes a dynamic of dependency and indebtedness. Not surprisingly, the lawyer feels intense resentment when Turkey tries to assert his dignity by stubbornly refusing to show gratitude for the gift.

It would appear, then, that Melville's narrator embodies both the decencies and the limitations of the older economic order. But to view him merely as an anachronism is to slight the complexity of his attitude. The narrator is not just a kindly if patronizing master; he also shares the instrumental ethos associated with rationalized capitalism and coexisting uneasily with his own lenient tendencies. This side of the narrator, the hard-headed side that places Bartleby out of his sight but within reach of his voice, regards his employees as tools or means to the end of making profit. He explains that he indulges Turkey's drinking because the copyist is "a most valuable person to me" during his periods of productivity, accomplishing "a great deal of work in a style not easily to be matched" (p. 42). He similarly describes Nippers as "a very useful man to me" (p. 43), and at first he even considers Bartleby "a valuable acquisition" because of his "incessant industry" (p. 53). In such moments, the lawyer seems to have no human connection to his scriveners other than as the buyer of their labor. They exist for him as a species of productive property and little else.

Hence a comprehensive view of the lawyer-narrator has to see him as a man divided between two economic perspectives, a lax one belonging to the household mode and a more calculating one suitable to the impersonal market system then establishing itself in America. The appearance of Bartleby at his law office aggravates this conflict and brings it into the open. About Bartleby himself very little is known: he materializes in response to a newspaper advertisement, and he doggedly "prefers not to" give an answer when the narrator asks him "who he was, or whence he came, or whether he had any relatives in the world" (p. 56). In his anonymity he suggests the faceless, unknown workers of the factory. Yet by refusing to conform to expectations, this total stranger forces the lawyer to keep making allowances for economically disadvantageous behavior, putting to the test his commitment to the personal values of the household system. When Bartleby declines to read copy, for example, the narrator initially feels outrage and is tempted to dismiss him. Shortly afterward he reflects that the scrivener's "eccentricities are involuntary. . . . I can get along with him. If I turn him away, the chances are that he will fall in with some less indulgent employer, and then he will be rudely treated, and perhaps driven forth miserably to starve" (p. 50).

The lawyer constantly vacillates between indignation and tolerance in dealing with Bartleby, between a businesslike attitude and a lenient one. His narrative thus exhibits on a personal level, in the way it was experienced by individual men and women, the struggle being played out in the larger culture as the unrestricted marketplace displaced the household as the center of economic life. Melville himself enacted a version of this struggle in *Moby-Dick*. The lawyer's fluctuations are reminiscent of the shifts of voice and attitude in the longer work, its waverings between a storytelling, "artisanal" mode and a more impersonal, distant posture toward the public. What appeared in *Moby-Dick* as a stylistic and structural discontinuity shows up here as a tension in the mind of a character. After finally ordering Bartleby to leave his premises, and finding that his command has been disregarded, the lawyer angrily advances on the scrivener and demands of him, "What earthly right have you to stay here? Do you pay any rent? Do you pay my taxes? Or is this property yours?" (p. 63). At this moment the narrator stands firmly on his prerogatives as a laissez-faire capitalist, disclaiming any obligation to his workers save the payment of their wages. He is so furious at Bartleby's obstinacy that he contemplates murdering him, but the thought of violence sets off a revealing train of associations in which he once again reverts to his old-fashioned loyalties.

> I remembered the tragedy of the unfortunate Adams and the still more unfortunate Colt in the solitary office of the latter; and how poor Colt, being dreadfully incensed by Adams, . . . was at unawares hurried into his fatal act. . . . Often it had occurred to me in my ponderings on the subject that had that altercation taken place in the public street, or at a private residence, it would not have terminated as it did. It was the circumstance of being alone in a solitary office, up stairs, of a building entirely unhallowed by humanizing domestic associations—an uncarpeted office, doubtless, of a dusty, haggard appearance—this it must have been, which greatly helped to enhance the irritable desperation of the hapless Colt. [Pp. 63–64]

Under the household regime, workmen regularly labored in their own homes or the homes of their masters as servants or apprentices, and the workplace was in fact hallowed by "humanizing domestic associations." Bartleby stirs up these ideas for the narrator not only because he defies the rational procedures of the law office but also because he insists upon living there as if it were "a private residence." Happening to visit Wall Street on a Sunday, the lawyer is startled to discover someone inside his chambers. A voice he recognizes as Bartleby's requests a moment's privacy, and when the narrator returns he finds the copyist's meager possessions—a blanket, a tin basin, even an improvised savings bank—secreted in his desk. "It is evident enough," he remarks, "that Bartleby has been making his home here, keeping bachelor's hall all by himself" (p. 55).

The narrator's ambivalence toward the market regime surfaces most dramatically after he has moved offices in an effort to escape Bartleby. He is tracked down at his new address by the lawyer who has inherited the unbudging scrivener and who holds him responsible for the man he left behind. Pressed to acknowledge Bartleby, the narrator declares that his former employee "is nothing to me—he is no relation or apprentice of mine, that you should hold me responsible for him" (p. 67). Cornered a second time, on this occasion by the wrathful landlord of his old building, he repeats his denial of any personal connection to the copyist: "I persisted that Bartleby was nothing to me—no more than to any one else" (p. 68). But these protests are followed soon enough by a change of heart. The narrator agrees under pressure to talk with Bartleby, and what he proceeds to say flatly contradicts his free-market sentiments; he invites the scrivener to come and live with him, as though he were speaking after all to "a relation or apprentice of mine." "Bartleby," he pleads, "will you go home with me now—not to my office, but my dwelling—and remain there till we can conclude upon some convenient arrangement for you at our leisure?" (p. 69). Moments before making this offer, the narrator mentions several possible jobs that might interest Bartleby more than copying, and in this too he betrays his attachment to an earlier phase of capitalism. He suggests positions such as clerk in a drygoods store, bartender, bill collector for merchants, and gentleman's traveling companion—positions which are limited and dependent, without much prospect of mobility, but which are also quite personal, requiring face-to-face dealings between employer and employee. What he does *not* propose is as significant as what he does: a job in a factory, the kind of work which in the American economy of 1853 was more and more frequently the lot of men (or women, as Melville shows in "The Tartarus of Maids") like Bartleby.

Melville's narrator sums up his reaction to his enigmatic employee by remarking that the news of Bartleby's imprisonment produced "a conflicting effect upon me" (p. 70). He emerges from his narrative as a man sharply at odds with himself, torn by conflicting allegiances to paternalism and to profits. Only partly at home in the new economic environment of impersonality, he is partly a victim of the same Wall Street spirit that jails Bartleby; indeed, their fates have striking similarities. Although the narrator is not physically deprived of liberty, he finds in the course of the story that his power to act has been drastically curtailed by the interference of his more practical and businesslike associates. On his own he becomes resigned to Bartleby, but his "professional reputation" suffers from the "uncharitable remarks" of other lawyers about the idle creature living in his office, and this threat to his livelihood completely undermines his resolve (p. 65). When he makes his final appeal to the scrivener, having consented to do so because he fears exposure in the papers, he seems no longer to have any will of his own. "If you do not go away from these premises before night," he exclaims to the copyist, "I shall feel bound—indeed, I *am* bound—to—to—to quit the premises myself!" (p. 69). The "energetic" landlord who has Bartleby arrested is representative of the new breed of capitalist (p. 70); he possesses none of the narrator's ambivalence about the decisive methods of the marketplace. Since the displeasure of men like the landlord is fatal to his ability to earn a living, the lawyer-narrator is "bound" to run away from a situation in which he feels helpless. He has as little genuine freedom of choice as an inmate of the Tombs.[6]

While Bartleby himself remains a mystery in the story, Melville provides ample reasons to associate him with the emergent market order. A "lean" and "penniless" hired clerk (p. 52), he belongs to the new class of workmen who have no personal ties to their employers: a class increasingly without choice or hope, for whom modern society is fast becoming a prison. Twenty years before Melville wrote "Bartleby," Tocqueville noted the emergence in America of such a class and offered an acute analysis of its relation to the "aristocracy" of capital. His comments deserve quotation at length for the light they shed on the lawyer's narrative.

> There is no real bond between [the rich] and the poor. . . .
> The workman is generally dependent on the master, but not
> on any particular master; these two men meet in the factory,
> but do not know each other elsewhere; and while they come

into contact at one point, they stand very far apart on all others. The manufacturer asks nothing of the workman but his labor; the workman expects nothing from him but his wages. The one contracts no obligation to protect nor to defend, and they are not permanently connected either by habit or duty. The aristocracy created by business rarely settles in the midst of the manufacturing population which it directs; the object is not to govern that population, but to use it. . . .

   The territorial aristocracy of former ages was . . . bound . . . to come to the relief of its serving-men and to relieve their distresses. But the manufacturing aristocracy of our age first impoverishes and debases the men who serve it and then abandons them to be supported by the charity of the public. . . . Between the workman and the master there are frequent relations, but no real association.[7]

Tocqueville's observations on the chasm between the rich and the poor, and the lack of contact between them, find their correlative in Melville's emphasis on walls. The Wall Street office of his story, with its high brick walls without and its folding screens within, corresponds to the social and spatial divisions generated by advanced capitalism and responsible for the mutual ignorance between the classes. The lawyer-narrator seems not unaware of the gulf of unfamiliarity separating "master and workman" in that he recognizes the difficulty of obtaining accurate information about some of the poor. He complains in the very first paragraph of his account that "Bartleby was one of those beings of whom nothing is ascertainable, except from the original sources, and, in his case, those are very small. What my own astonished eyes saw of Bartleby, *that* is all I know of him" (pp. 39–40). The irony of this lament is that the narrator himself has taken steps to ensure that he does *not* see people like the scrivener, even in the workplace; the partitions in his office, it will be recalled, are arranged so as to "isolate Bartleby from my sight."

According to Melville, "isolation from sight" is precisely the condition of the working class under the impersonal regimen of the market. Workmen are seen by their masters only in the factory or the office, if at all, and are otherwise hidden behind walls so that they are invisible to those who employ them. Although the narrator fails to realize his own complicity in his ignorance of Bartleby, he does have a sense at one point that the fate of the poor is to be excluded from view. When he happens across the copyist in his chambers on a Sunday, he is moved to melancholy reflections on the obscurity of poverty. "I remembered the bright silks and sparkling faces I had seen that day, in gala trim, swan-like sailing down the Mississippi of Broadway; and I contrasted them with the pallid copyist, and thought to myself, Ah, happiness courts the light, so we deem the world is gay; but misery hides aloof, so we deem that misery there is none" (p. 55).

This perception, that the poor are unseen and their sufferings unacknowledged, is immediately dismissed by the lawyer as the chimera "of a sick and silly brain" (p. 55). Nevertheless, the insight lies at the very heart of Melville's story, with its proliferation of enclosures and its eventual imprisonment, or physical removal from sight, of the title character. One of the starker ironies of the lawyer's narrative occurs when Bartleby decides to do no more copying and the narrator, looking "steadfastly" at his eyes, concludes that weeks of diligence have "temporarily impaired his vision" (p. 59). In fact Bartleby seems to be the only person in the story who is able to "see" what is going on in nineteenth-century America, who comprehends the growing isolation and loss of freedom of the working poor—a condition for which his dead-wall revery can be taken as a metaphor. As he says when the lawyer tries to cheer him up in prison, "I know where I am" (p. 71). On a later visit to the Tombs, the narrator finds the wasted copyist huddled by a wall in the yard and reports that "his dim eyes were open; otherwise he seemed profoundly sleeping" (p. 73). Bartleby the scrivener dies with his eyes open.

Melville's tale is concerned, then, with the invisibility of one class to another, a situation against which the lawyer-narrator uncertainly protests but in which he finally acquiesces, reluctantly approving the landlord's firmness in having Bartleby hauled off to prison. One even gets the impression from the story that this invisibility extends into the structure of the city: in other words, that the marketplace has imposed its "rationality" on the disposition of urban space. As Tocqueville pointed out, the modern businessman, unlike the master of the past, seldom resides in proximity to the workmen he employs. The nineteenth century witnessed the emergence of class neighborhoods and the gradual "ghettoization" of the poor as better-off families hastened to evacuate the urban center for the periphery.[8] The New York of Melville's narrator evidently permits a prosperous resident to travel from his home to his place of work without ever encountering a lower-class neighborhood or even setting eyes on a workman outside the office. The city appears to consist of a downtown commercial district which is crowded by day and uninhabited at night ("Of a

Sunday, Wall Street is deserted as Petra; and every night of every day it is an emptiness" [p. 55]); a long thoroughfare lined with shops, "the Mississippi of Broadway"; and outlying areas such as Manhattanville, Harlem, or Astoria where the affluent live and to which the lawyer flees after his last unsuccessful plea to Bartleby ("I drove about the upper part of the town and through the suburbs, in my rockaway" [p. 70]). Workmen and their families, once part of the everyday life of the master, have disappeared entirely from the middle-class field of vision. Confinement in the Tombs seems but the logical conclusion to an economic revolution which segregates and walls off from view the impoverished workers of the city.

Melville's distress over this development indicates how close he is in some regards to mid-nineteenth-century English writers, although "Bartleby" is also an illustration of his radical dissent from the basic optimism and backward-looking solutions of a Dickens or a Carlyle. The lawyer's narrative can be considered his Americanization of "the condition-of-England question," a fictional restatement of the problem Carlyle had first addressed in *Chartism* (1839): "Why are the Working Classes discontented; what is their condition, economical, moral, in their houses and their hearts?"[9] English novelists from Dickens to George Eliot responded to this question by deploring the mutual hostility and suspicion which had soured relations between the classes. A character in Benjamin Disraeli's *Sybil, or The Two Nations* (1845) declares that England's rich and poor are "two nations; between whom there is no intercourse and no sympathy; who are as ignorant of each other's habits, thoughts, and feelings, as if they were dwellers in different zones, or inhabitants of different planets; who are formed by a different breeding, are fed by a different food, are ordered by different manners, and are not governed by the same laws."[10] English writers commonly saw their own role as one of bridging this gulf of separation through literature. By displaying the inner lives of the poor to middle-class readers, they felt that they could help to restore a spirit of trust and caring among the classes.[11]

Melville has no such faith in his audience or in the power of literature to make available what lies inside the hearts and houses of alien beings like the scrivener. On the contrary, he regards literature itself as class-bound, written by and for the relatively privileged, and he despairs of overcoming the walls separating the rich and the poor. The first paragraph of the lawyer's narrative acknowledges the impossibility of composing a detailed portrait of the copyist:

The nature of my avocations, for the last thirty years, has brought me into more than ordinary contact with what would seem an interesting and somewhat singular set of men, of whom, as yet, nothing that I know of, has ever been written— I mean, the law-copyists, or scriveners. I have known very many of them, professionally and privately, and, if I pleased, could relate divers histories, at which good-natured gentlemen might smile, and sentimental souls might weep. But I waive the biographies of all other scriveners, for a few passages in the life of Bartleby, who was a scrivener, the strangest I ever saw, or heard of. While, of other law-copyists, I might write the complete life, of Bartleby nothing of that sort can be done. I believe that no materials exist, for a full and satisfactory biography of this man. It is an irreparable loss to literature. [P. 39]

The "good-natured gentlemen" and "sentimental souls" of this passage are remindful of the conventional "kindly reader" invoked in scores of English novels and counted on to feel sympathy for the sufferings of the lower orders. Bartleby constitutes a reproach to this reading public precisely by remaining outside its ken, an enigma about whom nothing satisfactory can be written because little or nothing can be known. In his opacity he forces Melville's audience to experience its own complicity in the social fragmentation engendered by the rational marketplace. Since "Bartleby" is told from the point of view of the lawyer, the reader is never permitted access to the interior thoughts of "the chief character . . . presented" in the narrative (p. 40). In Melville's "Story of Wall Street," a site of divisions, screens, and windows that only offer views of walls, the most impenetrable barrier of all is the one which stands between the curious reader and the private world of the scrivener. The turnkey at the Tombs calls Bartleby "the silent man" (p. 72), and Melville's point is that the class or group he represents does not speak—they have no voice—in the histories read and written by the middle class. They are not heard in texts just as they have been systematically eliminated from sight in the economy. As the lawyer-narrator observes, "It is an irreparable loss to literature."

The tragedy of "Bartleby" is the unknowability of the human, a consequence of the growth of the capitalist market and the widening rift between the classes. "We are blind to the real sights of this world," Melville wrote in *Redburn* (1849); "deaf to its voice; and dead to its death." [12] These words were inspired by the youthful Melville's exposure to English poverty as a merchant seaman in Liverpool, but

"Bartleby" is a story about America, and its tragedy is American. The lawyer-narrator refers to two background events in the course of his narrative, and the references seem intended to emphasize the nation's betrayal of "that unshackled, democratic spirit of Christianity" which Melville identified with the promise of the New World.[13] The lawyer discovers Bartleby in his office on a Sunday when he had planned to hear a celebrated minister preach at Trinity Church; "somehow," he muses afterward, "the things I had seen disqualified me for the time from church-going" (p. 56). The second background occurrence is an election day. Preoccupied with his own troubles, the narrator mistakes a stranger's bet on the outcome of the vote for an allusion to the scrivener before realizing that "the words I had overheard bore no reference to Bartleby" (p. 62). Indeed, neither Christianity nor democracy seems to bear very much relevance to the copyist. According to an unconfirmed rumor appended to the lawyer's narrative, the scrivener was employed for a time in the Dead Letter Office at the nation's capital in Washington. One implication among many is that the ideal of the United States as a Christian republic, a land of freedom and opportunity for the common man, has become a dead letter.

Two years after "Bartleby" Melville returned to the subject of class relations in a story which carries to conclusion the pessimism lurking just beneath the surface of the lawyer's tale. "The Paradise of Bachelors and the Tartarus of Maids," a diptych or two-part story, presents a much darker picture of the "two nations" theme and of the economic arrangements simultaneously linking and isolating the classes. The rich and the poor in this work are literally inhabitants of different countries, England and America, and they are physically separated by the structural division of the text into two apparently disparate sections. In the first part of the story, the narrator visits the Temple Bar of London, where he dines sumptuously on a feast of endless courses. The lawyers, he learns, are all bachelors, and as he gorges himself on food and drink, he is moved to reflect that "the thing called pain, the bugbear styled trouble—those two legends seemed preposterous to their bachelor imaginations. . . . Pain! Trouble! As well talk of Catholic miracles. No such thing" (p. 209).[14] The second half of the story recounts a winter visit by the same narrator to a mill situated not far from "Woedolor Mountain" in Massachusetts. A tour of the factory reveals row upon row of young women seated beside enormous machines, their faces pale and emaciated like the scrivener's. Freedom is extinct in this new kind of workplace, where machinery, "that vaunted slave of humanity," is "menially served by human beings" (p. 215). There seems to be no connection whatever between the Tartarus of Maids and the prosperous attorneys of the Temple Bar, between labor and capital, until it turns out that the mill is owned by an elderly bachelor known to his employees as "Old Bach." The comfort and plenty of the lawyers are made possible by the "pain" and "trouble" of the factory girls: by the deprivation which is never seen—whose very existence is denied—by those who profit from it. The two panels of the diptych, though divided, form but a single story.

The commodity produced by the factory in "The Tartarus of Maids" is paper, the sheets of foolscap on which Melville inscribes his fictions and the reader reads them. The Massachusetts paper mill is the point of origin for the "dead letters" of "Bartleby," the place where literature begins in an act of exploitation. Melville's conviction is strong in the diptych that reading and writing, even using language to express oneself verbally, have been monopolized by the more fortunate of the two nations: whereas the bachelors pass their evenings exchanging stories, "the human voice" has been "banished" from the factory, and the girls who work there have "eyes supernatural with unrelated misery" (p. 215). The suggestion that literature is contaminated by its association with privilege is more muted in "Bartleby," but it is unmistakably present even as Melville attempts to align his story with the voiceless working class. Bartleby's refusal to write has been interpreted as a portent of his creator's abandonment of fiction four years later,[15] but what really seems to be at stake in the tale is not so much writing per se as a particular kind of writing which Melville identifies with copying. To "copy" is to write realistic fiction, fiction that flatters the assumptions of the reading public by naturalizing or legitimating the existing state of affairs. Writing as copying accepts the social relations peculiar to rationalized capitalism as given and inevitable, portraying the status quo as the only possible "reality." At the end of the lawyer's narrative, he is asked by the grubman at the Tombs whether Bartleby is "a gentleman forger" like the notorious Monroe Edwards (p. 72). Forgers of course are people who make their livings with their pens, and in Melville's view copying or writing realism is little better than forgery in that it presents history as nature, the conventional as the inescapable. It is a species of counterfeiting which palms off the arbitrary and "false" as the permanent and "true."

Melville, however, refuses to write such fiction; he would "prefer not to." Instead he writes "Bartleby," a text that confounds the expectations of his audience by intensifying rather than abating the inaccessibility of the poor. By not abridging the distance between the two nations, between the scrivener on the one side and his readers on the other, Melville ensures that Bartleby will always seem a figure of strangeness to the "sentimental souls" and "good-natured gentlemen" who comprise his public. He seeks to make his readers aware that the social arrangements of the market system, arrangements in which they themselves are thoroughly implicated, are neither rational nor natural but fantastic. In "Bartleby" he creates a vision of the world of Wall Street so singular and bizarre as to expose the reality of class relations under capitalism as an absurdist fiction.

The sense of hopelessness in "Bartleby" flows from Melville's suspicion—perhaps it is already his belief—that the effort to free literature from its alliance with social and economic power is an exercise in futility. To write fiction subversive of the current order of things is to resign onself to the composition of texts without readers; this, surely, is one more meaning of the phrase "dead letters." But the phrase has still another meaning which bears more directly on Melville as author than on his audience. "Bartleby" is his first published work in which there is no autobiographical character: the "I" addressing us is not, like Ishmael, someone who speaks for his creator, and Melville the writer seems wholly removed from his fiction. Although the lawyer's vacillations recall the changes of narrative voice in *Moby-Dick*, the tale itself is not the product of an authorial consciousness torn between openness and concealment. Melville makes no effort here to achieve immediacy by putting the inner workings of the text on display. Rather, he positions himself vis-à-vis the reader much as Bartleby stands with respect to the lawyer: as an absence, an inscrutable blank wall. He disavows the possibility of a personal author-audience relation, taking the alienation of the working class as a figure for his own estrangement from the public. "I want nothing to say to you," Bartleby declares when the lawyer visits him in prison (p. 71). In these words, practically the last spoken by the scrivener, it is indeed possible to sense Melville's long withdrawal from fiction and to understand the significance of "dead letters" as a literature without authorial presence.

Afterword

Toward the end of his life, as his productivity waned and his antipathy toward the public intensified, Hawthorne found himself strongly drawn to the figure of Henry D. Thoreau. Although the two Concordians had never been intimate, Hawthorne had always had a high regard for Thoreau as a writer of unshakeable integrity; when the younger man was dying in 1862, he visited his sickroom and then attended his funeral with Sophia. It was Thoreau who had given him the idea for a story about the elixir of life, and Hawthorne was working on a version of this romance—one of several he started but failed to complete in this period—when he himself died two years later. He had planned to pay tribute to Thoreau by introducing the unfinished manuscript with a sketch of his former neighbor. "It seems the duty of a live literary man," he explained to his publisher, "to perpetuate the memory of a dead one, when there is such fair opportunity as in this case—but how Thoreau would scorn me for thinking that *I* could perpetuate *him*! And I don't think so."[1]

There is diffidence in this, and self-denigration too. Hawthorne had spent his career searching for some way to accommodate his commitment to the truth, his democratic beliefs, and his need to write for a living. Along with Melville, he had entertained the possibility that the mass public would support authors of genius. The "trade of literature," he had hoped, would prove as rewarding, and far less humiliating, than the precapitalist system of patronage. Thoreau represented a different course for the American writer, one that must have seemed prescient to the Hawthorne of the 1860s. The author of *Walden* put little trust in either democracy or the marketplace. He had sternly refused to conciliate the common reader, and he had dismissed the "great heart" of the many in favor of "a majority of one."[2]

The Civil War destroyed Hawthorne's faith in the people's judgment, but it was the disappointing reception of his fiction that mocked his hopes for an understanding popular audience and drove him toward an intransigence like Thoreau's. Only one of his published works brought him any financial security at all, and this was not a novel but the campaign biography of his college friend, Franklin Pierce, which he composed immediately following Pierce's nomination for the presidency in 1852. The memoir recapitulates the dilemma Hawthorne faced throughout his creative life. It bears testimony, not simply to the unblemished character of its subject, but also to the discernment of the multitude in advancing him in government. Hawthorne writes glowingly of Pierce's rapport with the public and attributes his success to "the influence of a great heart pervading the general heart, and throbbing with it in the same pulsation." Pierce's speeches evince "a genuine respect for the people," being innocent of any intent to cajole or deceive; hence his triumphs have been "as creditable to his audiences as to himself."[3]

The irony of all this is that Hawthorne undertook the *Life of Franklin Pierce* precisely in order to escape dependency on the democratic public. Though he stated in the preface that writing the biography was a distraction from "his customary occupations,"[4] in fact he originated the idea and saw in it the promise of deliverance from the uncertainties of the literary marketplace. He knew that if elected Pierce would show his gratitude with a lucrative patronage appointment. The new President offered him the hugely profitable consulship at Liverpool, and for several years the post spared Hawthorne further efforts to satisfy a popular taste from which he felt increasingly estranged.

The Marble Faun (1860), his last complete romance, reveals the extent of Hawthorne's disenchantment with his audience. Particularly in the brief "Conclusion," the book bristles with an aggression toward the reader that seems scarcely compatible with any wish to sell one's writing. Hawthorne introduces the romance with a curious note in which he remarks on his long absence from the public, insists that he has always meant his fictions not for the uncaring mass but for some "all-sympathizing" friend, and speculates that this "Gentle

Reader" has passed away during his years abroad.[5] After such an opening, it is hard to tell just whom Hawthorne is writing for in the ensuing narrative. And he must have wondered the same thing himself when negative critical reaction obliged him to add a postscript to the second edition. In the final chapter Hawthorne had expressed the hope that "the gentle reader" (whom he resurrected for the purpose) would have the good sense not to demand "clearing up the romantic mysteries of a story." But reviewers and critics, including some of the most appreciative, objected to the tale's vagueness and pressured him to elucidate its obscurities. Hawthorne responded with a few pages of sarcastic prose in which he purports to "cross-examine" Hilda and Kenyon about the supposed riddles. Their replies, accompanied by "glance[s] of friendly commiseration at [his] obtuseness," succeed in making matters as "clear as a London fog." Kenyon's concluding comment, regarding the ears of Donatello, sums up the change in Hawthorne's attitude from the "Pretty good business!" of *The House of the Seven Gables* to the belligerence of *The Marble Faun*. With the statement, "On that point, . . . there shall be not one word of explanation," Hawthorne ends his career as a novelist with an echo of Hester Prynne before the Boston populace: alienated from his audience and defiantly unwilling to bare his soul in the marketplace.[6]

Yet an additional irony should be registered. The person standing in for the dissatisfied public and pressing Kenyon for explanations is none other than Hawthorne himself. Although he upbraids his audience for demanding clarification, he confesses to feeling "troubled with a curiosity similar to that which he has just deprecated on the part of his readers."[7] He is at once the aggrieved author and the exasperated critic of his work, out of patience with a species of storytelling that never quite manages to achieve the popular tone of the pen-and-ink men. Frustrated by his repeated failures in the marketplace, Hawthorne had finally reached the point where he cared almost as little for his fiction as did the mass public. He acknowledged as much in a letter written while completing *The Marble Faun*:

> My own opinion is, that I am not really a popular writer. . . .
> Possibly I may (or may not) deserve something better than
> popularity; but looking at all my productions, and especially
> this latter one, with a cold or critical eye, I can see that they do
> not make their appeal to the popular mind. It is odd enough,
> moreover, that my own individual taste is for quite another
> class of works than those which I myself am able to write.

Were he to encounter his stories in a book by a different writer, Hawthorne added, he doubted that he would have the perseverance to get through them.[8]

Melville came to the end of his own career as an active novelist three years before Hawthorne made this admission. His fiction from the fifties exhibits a steady movement toward authorial withdrawal, reflecting a growing sense of disaffection from both the public and his art. Works as diverse as *Pierre* (1852), "Benito Cereno" (1855), and *Israel Potter* (1855) all have in common a wish to suppress or conceal the writer's identity. Pierre's story, for example, is told by a first-person narrator who is never named and who does not appear as a participant in the events he chronicles. It has been proposed that this mysterious figure may be Pierre himself;[9] since the hero, an aspiring writer, commits suicide on the last page, this would truly make him an author from the dead. What is indisputable, at all events, is that the narrator shares with Melville a desire for anonymity. Desperate over the poor sales of his works, Melville had suggested to his English publisher that "it might not prove unadvisable to publish this present book anonymously, or under an assumed name: —'*By a Vermonter*' say," or, he continued in a footnote, "'*By Guy Winthrop.*'"[10]

"Benito Cereno" and *Israel Potter* follow a different strategy for rendering the author inaccessible or absent. Both are based on existing documents and quote or paraphrase extensively from other writers. The story derives from an episode related by an actual Amasa Delano in his *Narrative of Voyages and Travels* (1817) and reprints with only minor alterations some dozen pages of court records contained in the original. The novel has as its principal source a pamphlet entitled *The Life and Remarkable Adventures of Israel R. Potter* (1824), the memoir of a Revolutionary veteran who had hoped to win a pension with the story of his hardships. It also incorporates material from books on or by Revolutionary notables such as Ethan Allen and John Paul Jones. In both the novel and the tale, Melville attempts to delete himself from the text by reducing his role to that of a compiler or editor of other men's words.

Poor sales alone cannot account for this direction in Melville's work, although after *Moby-Dick* it was as evident to him as to Hawthorne that his fiction would never make him self-supporting. What underlies his disappearance as a writer is the realization that democratic capitalist culture is no more congenial for the artist than the aristocratic civilization of the past. *The Confidence-Man* (1857), his most devastating picture of commercial society, is also his farewell to the novel. Here Melville envisages a nightmare world where all men assume disguises and conceal their true identities in order to persuade other men to put trust in them. Far from nurturing a spirit of mutuality, as Ishmael had hoped, "the age of joint-stock companies" has legitimized a state of affairs in which chicanery and manipulation are the norm. As the P.I.O. man observes, "Confidence is the indispensable basis of all sorts of business transactions. Without it, commerce between man and man, as between country and country, would, like a watch, run down and stop." The author is in the same position as anyone else under the market regime who has goods to sell. He has to win the confidence of potential customers, in his case the reading public, to induce them to purchase his commodities. The multiple con men of Melville's novel are versions of the artist who tell stories to obtain money and use language, not to communicate truth, but to obfuscate their motives and ingratiate themselves with listeners.[11]

The essay on the *Mosses* foreshadowed this situation, but in 1850 Melville's resentment at the writer's plight was balanced by his democratic enthusiasm. He now regards the common reader and the literary work with Ahab-like antagonism. The language in which he tells his story constitutes a deliberate act of hostility toward the public: there is no other book in antebellum American literature that has a style so obscure and devious as this one. Syntax goes awry, double negatives accumulate, and clauses spin out of control until sense becomes elusive if not impenetrable. Passages like the following seem calculated to try the reader's patience:

> the merchant, though not used to be very indiscreet, yet, being not entirely inhumane, remained not entirely unmoved.

> But, upon the whole, it could not be fairly said that his appearance was unprepossessing; indeed, to the congenial, it would have doubtless been not uncongenial; while to others, it could not fail to be at least curiously interesting, from the warm air of florid cordiality, contrasting itself with one knows not what kind of aguish sallowness of saving discretion lurking behind it.

> By a brisk, ruddy-cheeked man in a tasseled traveling-cap, carrying under his arm a ledger-like volume, the above words were addressed to the collegian before introduced, suddenly accosted by the rail to which not long after his retreat, as in

a previous chapter recounted, he had returned, and there remained.[12]

One of the most provoking features of *The Confidence-Man* is the difficulty of determining the source of a given speech or story. Many of the embedded narratives are told at second or third hand, all but dissolving the connection between the anecdote and its original author. The tale of China Aster, for example, is recounted by Egbert in his role as Charlie and in the style of "the original story-teller" who is never named. The longing for absence, the desire to disavow ties to one's writing, is so palpable in this novel that it even extends to the level of sentences. In the last of the three quoted passages, Melville does not say that a particular man addressed the above words to someone else; he says, rather, by a man, the above words were addressed, making the words the subject of the sentence and relegating the speaker to a dependent clause. Other sentences drop the speaker altogether: "Then added as in soliloquy"; "At length, in a pained tone, spoke." Melville's curious way of reproducing dialogue is perhaps the most common and graphic example of orphaning the text. There are literally scores of exchanges in which language is detached from the speaking subject:

> "Sir," with unimpaired affability, producing one of his boxes, "I am pained to meet with one who holds nature a dangerous character."
> "Shocking, shocking!" nervously tucking his frayed cravat-end out of sight.
> "Suppose they did?" with a menacing air.
> "Why, then—then, indeed," respectfully retreating. . . .

From the context it is usually possible to infer who is speaking in these colloquies, but lines of dialogue sometimes float in space without being attributed to anyone in particular. Chapter 2 begins with nineteen "epitaphic comments, conflictingly spoken or thought," for which no specific source is identified.[13]

The rage and alienation noticeable everywhere in *The Confidence-Man* amount to an acknowledgment that the conditions of production and exchange emergent under capitalism permit no exception for the author. To Melville, the reader is an adversary, and the product of his own labor a commodity without a human origin. A number of American writers appear as confidence men aboard the *Fidèle*, among them some of Melville's most illustrious contemporaries. Hawthorne is portrayed as a one-legged, discharged custom-house officer who tells a story about adultery, Poe as a crazed beggar hawking a rhapsodical tract, and Emerson and Thoreau as the mystic Mark Winsome and his disciple Egbert. There are also allusions to and conversations about famous writers from other periods and countries, two of whom are discussed at length: Tacitus, the circumspect republican historian who lived during the Roman Empire, and Shakespeare, the equally guarded master of the great Art of Telling the Truth. Melville once believed that American men of letters were better off than those who did not have the benefit of political liberty. Writing to a friend in 1849, he stated, "I hold it a verity, that even Shakespeare was not a frank man to the uttermost. And, indeed, who in this intolerant Universe is, or can be? But the Declaration of Independence makes a difference." [14] The message of *The Confidence-Man* is that democracy and the marketplace have not improved the situation of the artist: the American writer is in the same boat as his predecessors.

If Hawthorne at the close of his career glances in Thoreau's direction, Melville might be said to look back to Emerson—the early Emerson for whom the world as commodity was *scoriae* or excrement. The last pages of *The Confidence-Man* center on an old man, a representative of the reading public, who desires "something for safety" and is given a chamber pot as a life-preserver. [15] Having tried to establish a monkey-rope connection with his audience, Melville has come to view the exchange relation as an excremental tie, a degradation from which his only wish is to escape. American romanticism yields up this final judgment by the writer in his confrontation with the marketplace: a literature exchangeable for dollars is a literature not of intimacy but of revulsion.

One last point remains to be noted. Hawthorne and Melville move toward authorial poses of distance and impersonality because of their estrangement from the market system; but in doing so, they are complicit in its ethos. The same observation can be made about Thoreau's retreat into unintelligibility, his uncompromising attitude toward the nineteenth-century reading public. The disappearance of the author from his art is a literary corollary to the passing of the household order, with its face-to-face relations and hand-made goods. A reified text like *The Confidence-Man*, from which the author has banished all reminders of his presence, mirrors the world of the modern economy, where objects are produced in factories and exchanges mediated by money. Like the modernist novel, market society thrives on indirection and impersonality. Is it unreasonable to suppose, then, that the perdurability of the masked and difficult works of American romanticism is itself a testimony to the power of the market?

Notes

Introduction

1. Fernand Braudel, *The Wheels of Commerce*, trans. Siân Reynolds (New York: Harper & Row, 1982), pp. 28–29, passim.

2. Christopher Clark, "Household Economy, Market Exchange and the Rise of Capitalism in the Connecticut Valley, 1800–1860," *Journal of Social History* 13 (Winter 1979): 173. On the household system, see also James A. Henretta, "Families and Farms: *Mentalité* in Pre-Industrial America," *William and Mary Quarterly* 35 (1978): 3–32; and Michael Merrill, "Cash Is Good to Eat: Self-Sufficiency and Exchange in the Rural Economy of the United States," *Radical History Review* 4 (Winter 1977): 42–71.

3. Michael Paul Rogin, *Fathers and Children: Andrew Jackson and the Subjugation of the American Indian* (New York: Alfred A. Knopf, 1975), p. 253. My discussion of the antebellum economy relies on Rogin and the following works: Richard D. Brown, *Modernization: The Transformation of American Life, 1600–1865* (New York: Hill & Wang, 1976); Clarence H. Danhof, *Change in Agriculture: The Northern United States, 1820–1870* (Cambridge, Mass.: Harvard University Press, 1969); Douglass C. North, *The Economic Growth of the United States, 1790–1860* (New York: W. W. Norton & Co., 1966); and George R. Taylor, *The Transportation Revolution, 1815–1860* (1951; rpt., New York: Harper & Row, 1968).

4. North, p. 210.

5. Taylor, pp. 388, 79, 325.

6. Clark, p. 171.

7. Taylor, pp. 396–98; Rogin, p. 252.

8. William Charvat, *Literary Publishing in America, 1790–1850* (Philadelphia: University of Pennsylvania Press, 1959), pp. 38–55.

9. John Tebbel, *A History of Book Publishing in the United States: The Creation of an Industry, 1630–1865* (New York: R. R. Bowker, 1972), pp. 207, 257–59.

10. Charvat, pp. 55–57; James D. Hart, *The Popular Book: A History of America's Literary Taste* (New York: Oxford University Press, 1950), pp. 67, 90.

11. Melville to Evert A. Duyckinck, letter of 12 February 1851, in *The Letters of Herman Melville*, ed. Merrell R. Davis and William H. Gilman (New Haven: Yale University Press, 1960), p. 121.

12. See Karl Polanyi, *The Great Transformation: The Political and Economic Origins of Our Time* (1944; rpt., Boston: Beacon Press, 1957).

13. Leo Marx, *The Machine in the Garden: Technology and the Pastoral Ideal in America* (New York: Oxford University Press, 1964); Henry Nash Smith, *Democracy and the Novel: Popular Resistance to Classic American Writers* (New York: Oxford University Press, 1978), esp. pp. 3–55; William Charvat, "Melville and the Common Reader," in *The Profession of Authorship in America, 1800–1870: The Papers of William Charvat*, ed. Matthew J. Bruccoli (Columbus: Ohio State University Press, 1968), pp. 262–82; Ann Douglas, *The Feminization of American Culture* (New York: Alfred A. Knopf, 1977), pp. 289–326. For a classic interpretation of English romanticism as an oppositional movement, see Raymond Williams, *Culture and Society, 1780–1950* (1958; rpt., New York: Harper & Row, 1966), pp. 30–48 ("The Romantic Artist").

14. Ralph Waldo Emerson, "The Method of Nature," in *Nature, Addresses, and Lectures*, vol. 1, *The Collected Works of Ralph Waldo Emerson*, ed. Robert E. Spiller and Alfred R. Ferguson (Cambridge, Mass.: Harvard University Press, 1971), p. 121; Emerson, "Spiritual Laws," in *Essays: First Series*, vol. 2, *The Collected Works of Ralph Waldo Emerson*, ed. Joseph Slater, Alfred R. Ferguson, and Jean Ferguson Carr (Cambridge, Mass.: Harvard University Press, 1979), p. 87. On Emerson as a critic of capitalism, see also Carolyn Porter, *Seeing and Being: The Plight of the Participant Observer in Emerson, James, Adams, and Faulkner* (Middletown, Conn.: Wesleyan University Press, 1981), pp. 57–118.

15. Henry D. Thoreau, "The Commercial Spirit of Modern Times," in *Early Essays and Miscellanies*, ed. Joseph J. Moldenhauer et al. (Princeton: Princeton University Press, 1975), pp. 115–18; Thoreau, *Walden*, ed. J. Lyndon Shanley (Princeton: Princeton University Press, 1971), p. 23.

16. Hawthorne to William D. Ticknor, letter of 19 January 1855, quoted in James R. Mellow, *Nathaniel Hawthorne in His Times* (Boston: Houghton Mifflin, 1980), p. 456; Thoreau, "Life without Principle," in *Reform Papers*, ed. Wendell Glick (Princeton: Princeton University Press, 1973), p. 158; Emerson, "Spiritual Laws," in *Essays: First Series*, p. 89; Melville, *White-Jacket; or The World in a Man-of-War*, vol. 5, *The Writings of Herman Melville*, ed. Harrison Hayford, Hershel Parker, and G. Thomas Tanselle (Evanston and Chicago: Northwestern University Press and Newberry Library, 1970), p. 192.

17. Hart, pp. 91–96; Mary Kelley, *Private Woman, Public Stage: Literary Domesticity in Nineteenth-Century America* (New York: Oxford University Press, 1984), pp. 3–27.

18. Hart, pp. 91–92. The term "feminine fifties" was coined by Fred Lewis Pattee. See his book, *The Feminine Fifties* (New York: D. Appleton Century Co., 1940).

19. G. P. Putnam to Hawthorne, letter of 1853, in Hart, p. 93.

20. This view of the Jacksonian era is drawn primarily from Marvin Meyers, *The Jacksonian Persuasion: Politics and Belief* (Stanford: Stanford University Press, 1957); Fred Somkin, *Unquiet Eagle: Memory and Desire in the Idea of American Freedom, 1815–1860* (Ithaca: Cornell University Press, 1967); and Danhof. Michael A. Lebowitz has challenged the idea that the Jacksonians were riven by ambivalence about the market revolution. He argues that most opposition to the new order came from declining groups like mechanics and Eastern farmers. See his essay "The Jacksonians: Paradox Lost?" in *Towards a New Past: Dissenting Essays in American History*, ed. Barton J. Bernstein (New York: Vintage Books, 1969), pp. 65–89.

21. Emerson, *The Journals and Miscellaneous Notebooks of Ralph Waldo Emerson*, ed. William H. Gilman et al. (Cambridge, Mass.: Harvard University Press, 1960–), 4:249; Thoreau, *Walden*, p. 119; Melville, *Redburn: His First Voyage*, vol. 4, *The Writings of Herman Melville*, ed. Harrison Hayford, Hershel Parker, and G. Thomas Tanselle (Evanston and Chicago: Northwestern University Press and Newberry Library, 1969), p. 165.

22. Emerson, "Thoreau," in *The Selected Writings of Ralph Waldo Emerson*, ed. Brooks Atkinson (New York: Modern Library, 1950), p. 898.

23. Ibid.

24. Emerson to William Henry Furness, letter of 6 August 1847, quoted in the "Historical Introduction" to *A Week on the Concord and Merrimack Rivers*, ed. Carl F. Hovde, William L. Howarth, and Elizabeth Hall Witherell (Princeton: Princeton University Press, 1980), p. 462. Charvat calls Thoreau a nonprofessional in *The Profession of Authorship in America*, p. 297.

25. Horace Greeley to Henry D. Thoreau, letter of 19 November 1848, in *The Correspondence of Henry David Thoreau*, ed. Walter Harding and Carl Bode (New York: New York University Press, 1958), p. 232.

26. Melville, *White-Jacket*, p. 192.

27. Melville to John Murray, letter of 15 July 1846, in *Letters of Herman Melville*, pp. 39–40.

28. Hawthorne to James T. Fields, letter of 1851, in Fields, *Yesterdays with Authors* (Boston, 1872), p. 48.

29. See Alexis de Tocqueville, *Democracy in America*, ed. Phillips Bradley, 2 vols. (1835, 1840; rpt., New York: Alfred A. Knopf, 1945), 2:82–83; and Richard Chase, *The American Novel and Its Tradition* (Garden City, N.Y.: Doubleday Anchor, 1957), esp. pp. 1–28.

30. This is Kelley's thesis (see n. 17).

31. Hawthorne to William D. Ticknor, letter of 1855, in Hart, p. 94; Hawthorne to Horatio Bridge, letter of 4 February 1850, in Mellow, p. 303.

32. Emerson, "Thoreau," in *Selected Writings*, p. 911.

33. Thoreau, "Gaining or Exercising Public Influence," in *Early Essays and*

Miscellanies, pp. 86–88; Thoreau, "Thomas Carlyle and His Works," in *Early Essays and Miscellanies,* p. 243; Thoreau, *A Week on the Concord and Merrimack Rivers,* pp. 367, 376, 96.

34. Thoreau, "Civil Disobedience," in *Reform Papers,* pp. 86–87.

35. Thoreau, *Walden,* p. 36.

36. On the dual nature of the commodity, see Karl Marx, *Capital: A Critique of Political Economy,* trans. Ben Fowkes, 2 vols. (New York: Vintage Books, 1977), 1:125–77.

37. See Georg Lukács, *The Theory of the Novel,* trans. Anna Bostock (Cambridge, Mass.: MIT Press, 1971); and Lukács, *Studies in European Realism,* trans. Edith Bone (London: Hillway Publishing, 1950). My understanding of Lukács's analysis of symbolism has been aided by Frederic Jameson, *Marxism and Form: Twentieth-Century Dialectical Theories of Literature* (Princeton: Princeton University Press, 1971), pp. 160–205.

38. Hawthorne, *The Scarlet Letter,* Centenary Edition of the Works of Nathaniel Hawthorne, ed. William Charvat et al. (Columbus: Ohio State University Press, 1962), 1:3.

Chapter 1

1. From *The Conduct of Life,* vol. 6, *The Complete Works of Ralph Waldo Emerson,* ed. Edward W. Emerson, Centenary Edition (Boston: Houghton Mifflin, 1903–4), p. 87. Additional references to this edition will be cited in the text and identified by the abbreviation *W* followed by volume and page number.

2. *Walden,* ed. J. Lyndon Shanley (Princeton: Princeton University Press, 1971), p. 173.

3. Daniel Aaron, *Men of Good Hope: A Story of American Progressives* (New York: Oxford University Press, 1951), p. 8.

4. From "The Method of Nature," in *The Collected Works of Ralph Waldo Emerson,* vol. 1, *Nature, Addresses, and Lectures,* ed. Robert E. Spiller and Alfred R. Ferguson (Cambridge, Mass.: Harvard University Press, 1971), p. 131. Additional references to this edition will be cited in the text and identified by the abbreviation *CW* followed by volume and page number.

5. Joel Porte examines some of Emerson's affinities with his age in *Representative Man: Ralph Waldo Emerson in His Time* (New York: Oxford University Press, 1979). Porte finds parallels between Emerson's temperamental pattern of expansion and deflation and the "spermatic economy" of Jacksonian banking and revivalism. See esp. pp. 247–82. Several other studies focus more directly on Emerson's economic thought. In an important essay, "American Romanticism and the Depression of 1837," William Charvat argues that Emerson was repelled by the materialism of the "new middle class, who speculated in land . . . and were turning us into a money-mad nation without value, without principles"; in *The Profession of Authorship in America, 1800–1870: The Papers of William Charvat,* ed. Matthew J. Bruccoli (Columbus:

Ohio State University Press, 1968), pp. 49–67; quotation from p. 62. Quentin Anderson claims that Emerson devised his conception of the imperial self in reaction against "a society in which self-definition had come close to being reduced to a quest for property." See Anderson's article, "Property and Vision in Nineteenth-Century America," *Virginia Quarterly Review* 54 (Summer 1978): 385–410 (quotation from p. 409). My own argument emphasizes Emerson's ambivalence toward the antebellum economy, his delight in as well as his disdain for the marketplace.

6. From the introductory lecture to the series "The Present Age," delivered December 4, 1839, in *The Early Lectures of Ralph Waldo Emerson*, vol. 3, *1838–1842*, ed. Stephen E. Whicher, Robert E. Spiller, and Wallace E. Williams (Cambridge, Mass.: Harvard University Press, 1959, 1964, 1972), pp. 190–91.

7. Thomas Jefferson, *Notes on the State of Virginia*, ed. Thomas Perkins Abernethy (New York: Harper Torchbooks, 1964), p. 157.

8. Marvin Meyers, *The Jacksonian Persuasion: Politics and Belief* (Stanford: Stanford University Press, 1957), p. 179; Andrew Jackson, "Farewell Address," in *Social Theories of Jacksonian Democracy*, ed. Joseph L. Blau (Indianapolis: Bobbs-Merrill, 1954), pp. 12–13.

9. *The Journals and Miscellaneous Notebooks of Ralph Waldo Emerson*, ed. William H. Gilman et al. (Cambridge, Mass.: Harvard University Press, 1960–), 7:268.

10. Morton J. Horwitz, *The Transformation of American Law, 1780–1860* (Cambridge, Mass.: Harvard University Press, 1977), p. 48; Karl Polanyi, *The Great Transformation: The Political and Economic Origins of Our Time* (1944; rpt., Boston: Beacon Press, 1957), pp. 72–73.

11. *The Journals and Miscellaneous Notebooks*, 5:331–32. William Charvat also cites this passage and says that the effect of the economic collapse was "to send Emerson deeper into his idealism" ("American Romanticism and the Depression of 1837," p. 63).

12. On *Nature*'s escalating development, see Richard Lee Francis, "The Architectonics of Emerson's *Nature*," *American Quarterly* 19 (1967): 39–53.

13. *Oxford English Dictionary*, s.v. *scoriae*; and see Norman O. Brown, *Life against Death: The Psychoanalytical Meaning of History* (Middletown, Conn.: Wesleyan University Press, 1959), esp. pp. 179–304.

14. Cf. Marc Shell, *The Economy of Literature* (Baltimore: Johns Hopkins University Press, 1978), p. 84.

15. See the essay "Farming," in *Society and Solitude*, vol. 7, *The Complete Works*, p. 148.

16. *The Early Lectures*, 2:66.

17. Meyers, p. vii.

18. Stephen E. Whicher writes of Emerson and *Nature*: "The aim of this strain in his thought is not virtue, but freedom and mastery." See *Freedom and Fate: An Inner Life of Ralph Waldo Emerson* (Philadelphia: University of Pennsylvania Press, 1953), p. 56.

19. See, for example, the collection edited by M. Thomas Inge, *Agrarianism in American Literature* (New York: Odyssey Press, 1969). "Farming" was first delivered in 1858 but not published until 1870, when it appeared as a chapter of *Society and Solitude*.

20. Thoreau, *Walden*, p. 207. Emerson was more sympathetic to Thoreau in essays written after Thoreau's death, such as the memorial address of 1862 and "Historic Notes of Life and Letters in New England" (1880). Bronson Alcott, in a journal entry for 1852, makes a pertinent observation on the differences between the two thinkers: "Emerson said fine things last night about Wealth, but there are finer things far to be said in praise of Poverty, which it takes a person superior to Emerson even to say worthily. Thoreau is the better man, perhaps, to celebrate that estate, about which he knows much, and which he wears as an ornament about himself—a possession that Kings and Caesars are too poor to purchase." From *The Journals of Bronson Alcott*, ed. Odell Shepard (Boston: Little, Brown, 1938), p. 261.

Chapter 2

1. Henry D. Thoreau, *Walden*, ed. J. Lyndon Shanley (Princeton: Princeton University Press, 1971). Page numbers included in the text refer to this edition.

2. Ralph Waldo Emerson, "Thoreau," in *The Selected Writings of Ralph Waldo Emerson*, ed. Brooks Atkinson (New York: Modern Library, 1950), p. 896. The standard view of *Walden*'s development is given by Walter Harding and Michael Meyer in their edition of *The New Thoreau Handbook* (New York: New York University Press, 1980), p. 51: "*Walden* may seem to begin in despair, but it ends in ecstasy."

3. Leo Marx has explored *Walden* from the perspective of pastoralism in *The Machine in the Garden: Technology and the Pastoral Ideal in America* (New York: Oxford University Press, 1964), pp. 242–65. Marx sees Thoreau's great foe as technology, the railroad in particular; I regard technology as simply one aspect of the market society that is his real adversary.

4. On the civic humanist tradition, see J. G. A. Pocock, *The Machiavellian Moment: Florentine Political Thought and the Atlantic Republican Tradition* (Princeton: Princeton University Press, 1975).

5. See Lukács's *History and Class Consciousness: Studies in Marxist Dialectics* (Cambridge, Mass.: MIT Press, 1971), pp. 83–222. Also relevant is Roland Barthes, *Mythologies*, trans. Annette Lavers (New York: Hill & Wang, 1972), esp. pp. 109–59. A valuable discussion of reification and American literature appears in Carolyn Porter, *Seeing and Being: The Plight of the Participant Observer in Emerson, James, Adams, and Faulkner* (Middletown, Conn.: Wesleyan University Press, 1981), pp. 23–53, passim. On reification in Thoreau, the best treatment is John P. Diggins, "Thoreau, Marx and the 'Riddle' of Alienation," *Social Research* 39 (1972): 571–98.

6. The question of whether American farmers were ever really self-sufficient

is much debated. Clarence H. Danhof, for one, has argued that the market orientation deplored by Thoreau did not come to dominate American agriculture until the nineteenth century. See Danhof's *Change in Agriculture: The Northern United States, 1820–1870* (Cambridge, Mass.: Harvard University Press, 1969).

7. Compare Thoreau's question in *A Week on the Concord and Merrimack Rivers,* ed. Carl F. Hovde, William L. Howarth, and Elizabeth Hall Witherell (Princeton: Princeton University Press, 1980), p. 382: "Is not Nature, rightly read, that of which she is commonly taken to be the symbol merely?"

8. Henry D. Thoreau, *Reform Papers,* ed. Wendell Glick (Princeton: Princeton University Press, 1973), p. 88. For a reading of *Walden* as a heroic text, see Stanley Cavell, *The Senses of Walden* (New York: Viking Press, 1972).

9. See Lewis P. Simpson, *The Man of Letters in New England and the South: Essays on the History of the Literary Vocation in America* (Baton Rouge: Louisiana State University Press, 1973), esp. pp. 3–31.

10. Compare Roland Barthes, p. 141: "The status of the bourgeoisie is particular, historical: man as represented by it is universal, eternal."

11. Alexis de Tocqueville, *Democracy in America,* ed. Phillips Bradley, 2 vols. (1835, 1840; rpt., New York: Vintage Books, 1945), 2:64.

12. Thoreau's outburst here brings to mind another prominent American author who was for a time his townsman: Nathaniel Hawthorne. In *The House of the Seven Gables* (1851), Hawthorne takes an equally dim—if rather more bemused—view of his potential audience. His image for the undiscriminating public, eager to devour whatever is available (including the latest literature) and always hungry for more, is little Ned Higgins, the Yankee schoolboy who patronizes Hepzibah's cent shop and feasts on gingerbread figures of everything from men to locomotives.

13. *Reform Papers,* p. 77.

14. Lukács, p. 86.

15. J. Lyndon Shanley, *The Making of "Walden": With the Text of the First Version* (Chicago: University of Chicago Press, 1957), pp. 57, 87; see also Lawrence Buell, *Literary Transcendentalism: Style and Vision in the American Renaissance* (Ithaca: Cornell University Press, 1973), pp. 309–10.

16. Compare Shanley, p. 182.

17. Harding and Meyer, p. 11.

18. Laurence Stapleton, ed., *H. D. Thoreau: A Writer's Journal* (New York: Dover Books, 1960), p. 107. Walter Harding discerns a strain of despair in Thoreau's journal for 1853–54 and speculates that he was discouraged because "his literary career seemed to have reached a stalemate." See Harding's *The Days of Henry Thoreau* (New York: Alfred A. Knopf, 1965), p. 329.

19. Shanley, p. 11.

20. See Shanley's "Historical Introduction" to the Princeton edition of *Walden,* p. 363.

Chapter 3

1. Nina Baym, *The Shape of Hawthorne's Career* (Ithaca: Cornell University Press, 1976), p. 107.

2. "Rappaccini's Daughter" appears in *Mosses from an Old Manse*, Centenary Edition of the Works of Nathaniel Hawthorne, ed. William Charvat et al. (Columbus: Ohio State University Press, 1974), 10:91–128. "Hawthorne and His Mosses" is reprinted in *Moby-Dick*, Norton Critical Edition, ed. Harrison Hayford and Hershel Parker (New York: W. W. Norton and Co., 1967), pp. 535–51. Page numbers included in the text refer to these two editions.

3. Alexis de Tocqueville, *Democracy in America*, ed. Phillips Bradley, 2 vols. (1835, 1840; rpt., New York: Alfred A. Knopf, 1945), 2:64.

4. *Knickerbocker Magazine* 9 (July 1837): 3, 8–9. An extended discussion of the New York literary scene, and of the debates over nationalism in literature, appears in Perry Miller, *The Raven and the Whale: The War of Words and Wits in the Era of Poe and Melville* (New York: Harcourt, Brace & World, 1956).

5. On these matters, see William Charvat, "The People's Patronage," in *The Profession of Authorship in America, 1800–1870: The Papers of William Charvat*, ed. Matthew J. Bruccoli (Columbus: Ohio State University Press, 1968), pp. 298–316.

6. *United States Magazine and Democratic Review* 17 (July 1845): 63–64.

7. *Democratic Review*, pp. 63–65.

8. The rise of professional critics, and some of the implications of this development for literature, are explored by Allon White, *The Uses of Obscurity: The Fiction of Early Modernism* (London: Routledge & Kegan Paul, 1981), esp. pp. 13–75. The reader should also consult the various essays by William Charvat collected in *The Profession of Authorship in America*.

9. *Democratic Review*, pp. 65–66.

10. *Democratic Review*, p. 63.

11. Edgar A. Dryden argues this in *Melville's Thematics of Form: The Great Art of Telling the Truth* (Baltimore: Johns Hopkins University Press, 1968), pp. 21–29, passim.

12. Ralph Waldo Emerson, *Representative Men* (1850), in *The Complete Works of Ralph Waldo Emerson*, ed. Edward W. Emerson (Boston: Houghton Mifflin, 1903–4), 4:215. This was the version of Shakespeare popularized by Coleridge in his various lectures on the playwright. In perfect illustration of Melville's thesis, some nineteenth-century readers suspected Shakespeare of being someone other than himself: they attributed his plays to Francis Bacon. Hawthorne, aptly enough, was later to write a preface for the volume in which Celia Bacon argued the case for her ancestor as the real author of Shakespeare's works.

13. Melville to John Murray, letter of 29 October 1847, in *The Letters of Herman Melville*, ed. Merrell R. Davis and William H. Gilman (New Haven: Yale University Press, 1960), p. 67. Also see William Charvat, "Literary Eco-

nomics and Literary History," in *The Profession of Authorship in America*, pp. 283–97, esp. p. 293.

14. Melville to Richard Henry Dana, Jr., letter of 1 May 1850, in *Letters of Herman Melville*, p. 106.

15. See Walter Benjamin's essay, "The Storyteller," for a relevant discussion of the loss of immediacy in narrative which resulted from the dissemination of the book. In *Illuminations*, ed. Hannah Arendt (New York: Schocken Books, 1969), pp. 83–110.

16. William Charvat, *Literary Publishing in America, 1790–1850* (Philadelphia: University of Pennsylvania Press, 1959), p. 9. Hawthorne specifically mentions the success of Eugene Sue in the preface to "Rappaccini's Daughter."

17. See Meade Minnigerode, *The Fabulous Forties, 1840–1850* (New York: G. P. Putnam's Sons, 1924), pp. 105–39.

18. Hawthorne to Evert Duyckinck, letter of 26 November 1843, quoted in J. Donald Crowley, "Historical Commentary," *Mosses from an Old Manse*, p. 511.

19. Nathaniel Hawthorne, *The Scarlet Letter*, Centenary Edition (Columbus: Ohio State University Press, 1962), 1:36. Also see Don Parry Norford, "Rappaccini's Garden of Allegory," *American Literature* 50 (1978): 167–86.

20. *Mosses from an Old Manse*, p. 34; Longfellow's review (1842) is reprinted in J. Donald Crowley, *Hawthorne: The Critical Heritage* (New York: Barnes & Noble, 1970), p. 81. Longfellow was one of several friendly critics who spoke of Hawthorne's "feminine" sensibility.

21. *Mosses from an Old Manse*, pp. 30–31.

22. The standard treatment of the Common Sense tradition in America is Terence Martin, *The Instructed Vision: Scottish Common Sense Philosophy and the Origins of American Fiction* (Bloomington: Indiana University Press, 1961). Roy R. Male describes Baglioni as a spokesman for philosophical materialism in *Hawthorne's Tragic Vision* (Austin: University of Texas Press, 1957), p. 59.

23. "Preface" to *Twice-told Tales*, Centenary Edition (Columbus: Ohio State University Press, 1974), 9:6.

24. Lionel Trilling has pointed out that with a few notable exceptions, admiration for Hawthorne's "blackness" has been confined to the twentieth century. See "Hawthorne in Our Time," in *Beyond Culture: Essays on Literature and Learning* (New York: Viking Press, 1968), pp. 179–208.

25. Hawthorne to James T. Fields, letter of 24 October 1863, quoted in Arlin Turner, *Nathaniel Hawthorne: A Biography* (New York: Oxford University Press, 1980), p. 382.

26. *The Scarlet Letter*, p. 162.

Chapter 4

1. Poe's review, "Tale Writing—Nathaniel Hawthorne," is reprinted in B. Bernard Cohen, ed., *The Recognition of Nathaniel Hawthorne: Selected Criticism since 1828* (Ann Arbor: University of Michigan Press, 1969), pp. 21–27; quotation from p. 21.

2. Hawthorne to George Hillard, letter of 20 January 1850, quoted in Arlin Turner, *Nathaniel Hawthorne: A Biography* (New York: Oxford University Press, 1980), p. 191.

3. Several recent critical studies have addressed the question of Hawthorne's relation to the literary marketplace, notably Henry Nash Smith, *Democracy and the Novel: Popular Resistance to Classic American Writers* (New York: Oxford University Press, 1978), pp. 16–34; and Nina Baym, *The Shape of Hawthorne's Career* (Ithaca: Cornell University Press, 1976). Both Smith and Baym see Hawthorne as affronting popular taste in *The Scarlet Letter*; their interpretations overlook his considerable interest in, and need for, popular acceptance. More accurate, in my view, is the judgment of William Charvat that "the artist was sometimes at his best when the two pressures—creative and social—were in equilibrium." See *The Profession of Authorship in America, 1800–1870: The Papers of William Charvat*, ed. Matthew J. Bruccoli (Columbus: Ohio State University Press, 1968), p. 297. Stephen Nissenbaum's "Introduction" to Nathaniel Hawthorne's *The Scarlet Letter and Other Writings* (New York: Modern Library, 1984), came to my attention too late for me to take his reading into account. Nissenbaum reaches some similar conclusions about Hawthorne's uneasy craving for public acclaim. See pp. vii–xlii. All quotations from *The Scarlet Letter* will be from the Centenary Edition of the Works of Nathaniel Hawthorne, ed. William Charvat et al. (Columbus: Ohio State University Press, 1962), vol. 1. Page numbers will be given parenthetically in the text.

4. Hawthorne's interest in spectatorship is usually taken to be a product of his philosophical questioning, in particular his concern with the epistemological problems raised by multiple perspectivism. See the readings by Richard H. Brodhead, *Hawthorne, Melville, and the Novel* (Chicago: University of Chicago Press, 1976), pp. 43–68; and John T. Irwin, *American Hieroglyphics: The Symbol of the Egyptian Hieroglyphics in the American Renaissance* (New Haven: Yale University Press, 1980), pp. 239–84.

5. *The House of the Seven Gables*, Centenary Edition (Columbus: Ohio State University Press, 1965), 2:32, 35. Additional page references are included parenthetically in the text.

6. These themes are treated at greater length in Chapter 5.

7. *Mosses from an Old Manse*, Centenary Edition (Columbus: Ohio State University Press, 1974), 10:33.

8. "Preface" to *The Marble Faun*, Centenary Edition (Columbus: Ohio State University Press, 1968), 4:2.

9. There is a relevant comment on writing and the stares of the mar-

ketplace in the diary of Bronson Alcott. An entry dated 12 January 1851 (a year after the publication of *The Scarlet Letter*) complains of the ordeal of putting one's thoughts into writing: "Perhaps a Diary is the most difficult feat of authorship. I should be too happy if I had before me the transcript of a single day. But the best refuses to be put into the pillory of words, and to be gazed at, as multitudes stare at culprits, and mock, in the market-place." See *The Journals of Bronson Alcott*, ed. Odell Shepard (Boston: Little, Brown, 1938), p. 236.

10. Several recent articles have emphasized this aspect of Hawthorne's novel. See in particular Michael Ragussis, "Family Discourse and Fiction in *The Scarlet Letter*," *ELH* 49 (Winter 1982): 863–88; and Louise K. Barnett, "Speech and Society in *The Scarlet Letter*," *ESQ* 29 (1983): 16–24.

11. Sophia Hawthorne to her mother, letter of 2 September 1849, quoted in Turner, p. 189.

12. *The Marble Faun*, p. 2.

13. Charvat, *The Profession of Authorship in America*, p. 6.

14. Ibid., p. 293.

15. E. A. Duyckinck, "On Writing for the Magazines," *United States Magazine and Democratic Review* 16 (May 1845): 455–60. Hawthorne would almost certainly have seen this article.

16. Citations to "The Old Manse" are from the Centenary Edition of *Mosses from an Old Manse*; page numbers in this paragraph refer to this edition.

17. The preface to *The Snow-Image* contains an almost identical expression of antagonism. Disputing the charge that he has been indiscreet in his introductions, Hawthorne writes: "I have been especially careful to make no disclosures respecting myself . . . which I was not perfectly willing my worst enemy should know." In *The Snow-Image and Uncollected Tales*, Centenary Edition (Columbus: Ohio State University Press, 1974), 11 : 3.

18. Hawthorne to James T. Fields, letter of 20 January 1850, in James T. Fields, *Yesterdays with Authors* (Boston, 1872), pp. 51–52.

19. On Hawthorne's dismissal from the customhouse, see Stephen Nissenbaum, "The Firing of Nathaniel Hawthorne," *Essex Institute Historical Collections* 114 (1978): 57–86.

20. "Preface," *Twice-told Tales*, Centenary Edition (Columbus: Ohio State University Press, 1974), 9 : 3.

21. Hawthorne to Richard Monckton Milnes, letter of 13 November 1854, quoted in Turner, p. 355. *Aesthetic Papers*, the volume edited by Elizabeth Peabody, also contained Hawthorne's story "Main-Street." James R. Mellow remarks that "Hawthorne seems to have regarded Thoreau . . . as a standing criticism of his own way of life." See *Nathaniel Hawthorne in His Times* (Boston: Houghton Mifflin, 1980), p. 259.

22. Hawthorne to Milnes, letter of 13 November 1854, in Turner, p. 355.

23. The rise of "symptomatic reading" in the nineteenth century (the term

comes from Louis Althusser) is discussed by Allon White, *The Uses of Obscurity: The Fiction of Early Modernism* (London: Routledge & Kegan Paul, 1981).

24. "Preface," *The Snow-Image and Uncollected Tales*, p. 4.

25. The phrase is a coinage of Roland Barthes. See "The Death of the Author," in *Image-Music-Text*, trans. Stephen Heath (New York: Hill & Wang, 1977), pp. 142–48.

Chapter 5

1. F. O. Matthiessen, *American Renaissance: Art and Expression in the Age of Emerson and Whitman* (New York: Oxford University Press, 1941), p. 332. For a recent defense of the ending, see Edwin M. Eigner, *The Metaphysical Novel in England and America: Dickens, Bulwer, Hawthorne, Melville* (Berkeley and Los Angeles: University of California Press, 1978), pp. 99–109.

2. William Charvat, "Introduction," *The House of the Seven Gables*, Centenary Edition of the Works of Nathaniel Hawthorne, ed. William Charvat et al. (Columbus: Ohio State University Press, 1965), 2:xx–xxii. All citations to *The House of the Seven Gables* will be from this edition; page references will be given parenthetically in the text.

3. Herman Melville, "Hawthorne and His Mosses," in *Moby-Dick*, Norton Critical Edition, ed. Harrison Hayford and Hershel Parker (New York: W. W. Norton & Co., 1967), pp. 542, passim.

4. On Hawthorne's use of the legendary in *The House of the Seven Gables*, see Richard H. Brodhead, *Hawthorne, Melville, and the Novel* (Chicago: University of Chicago Press, 1976), pp. 69–90.

5. Nathaniel Hawthorne, *The Scarlet Letter*, Centenary Edition (Columbus: Ohio State University Press, 1962), 1:46.

6. Nathaniel Hawthorne, "Preface," *Twice-told Tales*, Centenary Edition (Columbus: Ohio State University Press, 1974), 9:3.

7. "Preface," *Twice-told Tales*, Centenary Edition, p. 6; see also the letter to James T. Fields of 20 January 1850 in which Hawthorne describes the public as a "great gull." In Fields, *Yesterdays with Authors* (Boston, 1872), pp. 51–52.

8. Marcus Cunliffe suggests that his attacks on the Judge "throw light upon Hawthorne's complicated private defenses against worldly success." See Cunliffe's essay, "*The House of the Seven Gables*," in *Hawthorne Centenary Essays*, ed. Roy Harvey Pearce (Columbus: Ohio State University Press, 1964), p. 89.

9. Nathaniel Hawthorne, "Preface," *The Snow-Image and Uncollected Tales*, Centenary Edition (Columbus: Ohio State University Press, 1974), 11:4.

10. "Preface," *The Snow-Image and Uncollected Tales*, Centenary Edition, p. 4.

11. "Preface," *Twice-told Tales*, Centenary Edition, p. 6.

12. *The Scarlet Letter*, Centenary Edition, p. 43; see also Hawthorne to

Horatio Bridge, letter of 4 February 1850, quoted by Charvat, "Introduction" to the Centenary Edition of *The Scarlet Letter*, p. xv.

13. Whipple's review is cited in Bertha Faust, *Hawthorne's Contemporaneous Reputation: A Study of Literary Opinion in America and England, 1828–1864* (1939; rpt., New York: Octagon Books, 1968), pp. 71–72.

14. "Rappaccini's Daughter," *Mosses from an Old Manse*, Centenary Edition, p. 91.

15. Hawthorne to Horatio Bridge, letter of 22 July 1851, quoted by Charvat, "Introduction," *The House of the Seven Gables*, Centenary Edition, p. xvi.

16. My account follows Charvat, "Introduction," *The House of the Seven Gables*, Centenary Edition, pp. xv–xxviii. All quotations in this paragraph are from letters to Fields, pp. xxii, xviii.

17. Hawthorne to E. A. Duyckinck, letter of 27 April 1851, quoted by Charvat, "Introduction," *The House of the Seven Gables*, Centenary Edition, p. xxii.

18. See William P. Dillingham, "Structure and Theme in *The House of the Seven Gables*," *Nineteenth-Century Fiction* 14 (1959): 59–70.

19. "Hawthorne and His Mosses," Norton Critical Edition of *Moby-Dick*, p. 536.

20. See Terence Martin, *Nathaniel Hawthorne* (New York: Twayne Publishers, 1965), pp. 140–41.

21. Whipple's review appeared in *Graham's Magazine* 38 (June 1851): 467–68.

22. See Rudolph Von Abele, *The Death of the Artist: A Study of Hawthorne's Disintegration* (The Hague: Martinus Nijhoff, 1955).

Chapter 6

1. Herman Melville, *Moby-Dick*, ed. Charles Feidelson, Jr. (Indianapolis: Bobbs-Merrill, 1964). Page numbers given in the text refer to this edition.

2. Ralph Waldo Emerson, "The Young American," in *Nature, Addresses, and Lectures*, vol. 1, *The Collected Works of Ralph Waldo Emerson*, ed. Robert E. Spiller and Alfred R. Ferguson (Cambridge, Mass.: Harvard University Press, 1971), p. 239.

3. Emerson, "The Transcendentalist," in *Nature, Addresses, and Lectures*, p. 216.

4. Karl Marx, *Economic and Philosophical Manuscripts* (1844), in *Early Writings*, trans. Rodney Livingstone and Gregor Benton (Hammondsworth: Penguin Books, 1975), p. 331.

5. See the interpretation of *Moby-Dick* by Leo Marx in *The Machine in the Garden: Technology and the Pastoral Ideal in America* (New York: Oxford University Press, 1964), pp. 277–319.

6. Cf. Marc Shell, *The Economy of Literature* (Baltimore: Johns Hopkins University Press, 1978), pp. 83–85.

7. As Michael Paul Rogin points out, "*The Pequod* is the single ship in all of Melville's stories on which a product is made." See *Subversive Genealogy: The Politics and Art of Herman Melville* (New York: Alfred A. Knopf, 1983), p. 111.

8. Edgar A. Dryden discusses the book-whale analogy in *Moby-Dick* as evidence of Ishmael's wish to escape to the security of a fictional or literary world. See *Melville's Thematics of Form: The Great Art of Telling the Truth* (Baltimore: Johns Hopkins University Press, 1968), pp. 83–113.

9. I am paraphrasing Emerson's famous statement about Hawthorne: "Hawthorne invites his readers too much into his study, opens the process before them. As if the confectioner should say to his customers, Now let us make the cake." Cited in Larzer Ziff, *Literary Democracy: The Declaration of Cultural Independence in America* (New York: Viking Press, 1981), p. 37.

10. See Benjamin's essay on "The Storyteller," in *Illuminations*, ed. Hannah Arendt (New York: Schocken Books, 1969), pp. 83–110.

11. Melville even steps forward at one point to inform us of the exact time of his writing: "fifteen and a quarter minutes past one o'clock P.M. of this sixteenth day of December, A.D., 1851" (p. 475). The hand has thematic as well as formal significance in *Moby-Dick*; see, for example, chap. 94, "A Squeeze of the Hand."

12. On Melville's engagement with the reader, see A. Robert Lee, "*Moby-Dick*: The Tale and the Telling," in *New Perspectives on Melville*, ed. Faith Pullin (Kent: Kent State University Press, 1978), pp. 86–127.

13. See Georg Simmel, *The Philosophy of Money*, trans. Tom Bottomore and David Frisby (London: Routledge & Kegan Paul, 1978), p. 457.

14. Melville to Nathaniel Hawthorne, letter of 1? June 1851, in *The Letters of Herman Melville*, ed. Merrell R. Davis and William H. Gilman (New Haven: Yale University Press, 1960), pp. 127–28. See also Leon Howard, *Herman Melville: A Biography* (Berkeley and Los Angeles: University of California Press, 1967), p. 175.

15. Melville to Lemuel Shaw, letter of 6 October 1849, in *Letters of Herman Melville*, pp. 91–92.

16. Harrison Hayford suggests that the *Pequod*'s carpenter is a version of Melville in "Unnecessary Duplicates: A Key to the Writing of *Moby-Dick*," in Pullin, p. 160.

17. See, for example, the readings of *Moby-Dick* by Rogin, pp. 102–51; and Robert Zoellner, *The Salt-Sea Mastodon* (Berkeley and Los Angeles: University of California Press, 1973).

18. The best study of Melville's racial views is Carolyn L. Karcher, *Shadow over the Promised Land: Slavery, Race, and Violence in Melville's America* (Baton Rouge: Louisiana State University Press, 1980).

19. See the interpretation of Melville's work by Ann Douglas, *The Feminization of American Culture* (New York: Alfred A. Knopf, 1977), pp. 289–326 ("Herman Melville and the Revolt against the Reader").

20. An example of authorial absence in Melville's earlier fiction is the

anonymous scroll from *Mardi*, which offers detailed criticisms of Vivenza (the United States) and is indignantly torn to shreds by the natives.

21. I borrow the term from Roland Barthes, "The Death of the Author," in *Image-Music-Text*, trans. Stephen Heath (New York: Hill & Wang, 1977), pp. 142–48.

22. The quoted phrase is from "Hawthorne and His Mosses," in *Moby-Dick*, Norton Critical Edition, ed. Harrison Hayford and Hershel Parker (New York: W. W. Norton & Co., 1967), p. 542. On Ishmael's disguises, see Dryden, pp. 83–113; and Paul Brodtkorb, Jr., *Ishmael's White World: A Phenomenological Reading of Moby Dick* (New Haven: Yale University Press, 1965). My discussion of authorial disappearance in *Moby-Dick* is also indebted to Cindy Weinstein, who explored similar ideas with me in her senior thesis on Melville, "Writing a Book without an Author," Brandeis University, 1982.

23. The review from *The Spectator* is reprinted in Herman Melville, *Moby-Dick*, ed. Charles Child Walcutt (Toronto: Bantam Books, 1967), pp. 547–48.

24. An incident in Ishmael's narrative foreshadows the later phrase. In chap. 71, "The Jeroboam's Story," Ahab remembers a letter intended for the chief mate of the passing ship, who has been killed by Moby Dick. "Of such a letter," Melville comments, "Death himself might well have been the post-boy" (p. 443).

25. See Nina Baym, "Melville's Quarrel with Fiction," *PMLA* 94 (October 1979): 909–23.

Chapter 7

1. Quotations are from Herman Melville, *Great Short Works of Herman Melville*, ed. Warner Berthoff (New York: Harper & Row, 1970). Page references are given parenthetically in the text.

2. On the theme of confinement in "Bartleby," see Marvin Fisher, *Going Under: Melville's Short Fiction and the American 1850s* (Baton Rouge: Louisiana State University Press, 1977), pp. 179–99.

3. See Pearl Chesler Solomon, *Dickens and Melville in Their Time* (New York: Columbia University Press, 1975), pp. 7–42, for a thorough discussion of the Dickensian strain in Melville's story.

4. "Chancery" refers to a body of custom that supplemented statute law and mitigated its harshness. The office of Master in Chancery was abolished as a result of the general movement to rationalize the legal system; the narrator's association with the post is further evidence of his old-fashioned outlook.

5. The story of this change has been told many times; a good recent summary is Paul E. Johnson, *A Shopkeeper's Millennium: Society and Revivals in Rochester, New York, 1815–1837* (New York: Hill & Wang, 1978), pp. 15–61.

6. At one point the narrator reports that he has been reading Jonathan Edwards's treatise on *Freedom of the Will*, which persuades him that his troubles have been predestinated; Bartleby has been "billeted upon me," he says, "for

some mysterious purpose of an all-wise Providence" (p. 65). But the narrative itself suggests that the loss of freedom experienced by both the lawyer and his scrivener has more to do with the new economic forces than with the decrees of the Almighty.

7. Alexis de Tocqueville, *Democracy in America*, ed. Phillips Bradley, 2 vols. (1835, 1840; rpt., New York: Alfred A. Knopf, 1945), 2:170–71.

8. See Johnson, pp. 48–55; and Steven Marcus, *Engels, Manchester and the Working Class* (New York: Random House, 1974), pp. 28–66.

9. Thomas Carlyle, *Carlyle: Selected Works, Reminiscences and Letters*, ed. Julian Symons (Cambridge, Mass.: Harvard University Press, 1970), p. 264.

10. Benjamin Disraeli, *Sybil, or The Two Nations* (London: Thomas Nelson & Sons, 1957), p. 85.

11. On the contrast between Melville and his English contemporaries, see Stephen Zelnick, "Melville's 'Bartleby': History, Ideology, and Literature," *Marxist Perspectives* 2 (Winter 1979–80): 74–92.

12. Herman Melville, *Redburn: His First Voyage*, vol. 4, *The Writings of Herman Melville*, ed. Harrison Hayford, Hershel Parker, and G. Thomas Tanselle (Evanston and Chicago: Northwestern University Press and Newberry Library, 1969), p. 293.

13. The quotation is from "Hawthorne and His Mosses," in *Moby-Dick*, Norton Critical Edition, ed. Harrison Hayford and Hershel Parker (New York: W. W. Norton & Co., 1967), p. 546.

14. The story is reprinted in Berthoff, ed., *Great Short Works of Herman Melville*; page numbers refer to this edition.

15. Leo Marx examines "Bartleby" in relation to Melville's career as a writer in "Melville's Parable of the Walls," *Sewanee Review* 61 (1953): 602–27.

Afterword

1. Hawthorne to James T. Fields, letter of 24 October 1863, quoted in James R. Mellow, *Nathaniel Hawthorne in His Times* (Boston: Houghton Mifflin Co., 1980), p. 559.

2. Henry D. Thoreau, *Reform Papers*, ed. Wendell Glick (Princeton: Princeton University Press, 1973), p. 74.

3. Nathaniel Hawthorne, *Life of Franklin Pierce* (1852), in *The Complete Writings of Nathaniel Hawthorne* (Boston: Houghton Mifflin, 1900), 17:124, 161–62, 190.

4. *Life of Pierce*, p. 75.

5. Nathaniel Hawthorne, *The Marble Faun: Or, The Romance of Monte Beni*, Centenary Edition of the Works of Nathaniel Hawthorne, ed. William Charvat et al. (Columbus: Ohio State University Press, 1968), 4:1–2.

6. *The Marble Faun*, pp. 455, 464–65, 467; *The House of the Seven Gables*, Centenary Edition (Columbus: Ohio State University Press, 1965), 2:319.

7. *The Marble Faun*, p. 464.

8. Hawthorne to James T. Fields, letter of 11 February 1860, cited in James T. Fields, *Yesterdays with Authors* (Boston, 1872), pp. 87–88.

9. See Raymond J. Nelson, "The Art of Herman Melville: The Author of *Pierre*," *Yale Review* 59 (1970): 197–214.

10. Melville to Richard Bentley, letter of 16 April 1852, in *The Letters of Herman Melville*, ed. Merrell R. Davis and William H. Gilman (New Haven: Yale University Press, 1960), p. 151.

11. Herman Melville, *The Confidence-Man: His Masquerade*, Norton Critical Edition, ed. Hershel Parker (New York: W. W. Norton & Co., 1971), pp. 153, 111.

12. *The Confidence-Man*, pp. 17, 121, 39.

13. *The Confidence-Man*, pp. 28, 120, 94, 102, 96, 5.

14. Melville to Evert A. Duyckinck, letter of 3 March 1849, in *Letters of Herman Melville*, p. 80.

15. *The Confidence-Man*, p. 216.

Index